T0105008

A LAYMAN'S
CHRISTIANITY

Ken Dickason

WestBow
PRESS
A DIVISION OF THOMAS NELSON

WestBow Press books may be ordered through booksellers or by contacting:

WestBow Press
A Division of Thomas Nelson
1663 Liberty Drive
Bloomington, IN 47403
www.westbowpress.com
1-(866) 928-1240

ISBN: 978-1-4497-0545-9 (sc)
ISBN: 978-1-4497-0547-3 (hbk)
ISBN: 978-1-4497-0546-6 (e)

Library of Congress Control Number: 2010935779

Printed in the United States of America

WestBow Press rev. date: 11/3/2010

I want to dedicate this book to the two people who have contributed the most to make me who I am (please don't hate them for it).

To Dad, who taught me how to think like a Christian, and to Mama, who taught me how to live like a Christian.

To both parents, who taught me what it was how to have faith, hope and love. To have faith that God will see through the most difficult of times; to have outrageous hope in the biggest things, knowing that God can do all things and do all things well; to have love for God, even when life is easy and it seems like there is no "need" for God.

I love you guys.

Contents

Forward

Anytime a man or woman reads a book by a new author, they most likely want to know the author's credentials. Well, this should be very simple in my case: I have none. Still want to read on? Good.

I have no formal education in religious studies. I did graduate from a Christian high school, but that hardly qualifies one for the pastorate. I do have a college education, but so do a lot of people in the world. I just wanted to write a book, so I did.

I'm going to be honest with you, though you may have purchased this book in the "Christian Living" section, or as a "self-help" book, it's not a self-help book at all.

Frankly, I don't think you can do the things in this book "by yourself." I can't. I don't. In fact, what I will be writing will fall under the "do what I say, not what I do" category, because I cannot claim that I put every little bit into practice. For anyone to live a Christian life takes the redemptive work of the Holy Spirit.

A dog cannot act like a cat; it is against its nature. Neither should we expect a nonbeliever to act in accordance with Christian tenets, because it is against their nature as well.

One thing I want you, the reader, to do is to keep a Bible close at hand while you read this book. It is possible that I could be wrong in some areas, but you need to rely on your Bible to prove the truth or disprove the lie of what I am saying.

There should be nothing new in this book. Perhaps the perspective is different from other books, but if the book holds true to biblical principles, then it's not because I am someone special that hears things from God that He hasn't told anyone else. I have gone to great lengths to make sure that what is said in this book matches up with the Bible. If what I say cannot be confirmed by the Bible, then I am probably wrong.

What this book is about

It's about 170 pages long.

Haha; funny little man.

This book is a bunch of barely-related essays about different issues that we Christians have to deal with, ranging from faith to grief. I wrote this book with one thing in mind: what is the type of Christianity that I want to believe in? How do I want to live my life as a follower of Christ? It is in this vein that I write, hoping that you will have many of the same questions that I have about how to live as a Christian, and I hope that you will consider what I say, even though I try to make rather corny jokes along the way.

To those reading this book who are not Christians, but are curious to hear what it really means to be a Christian, I hope you'll finish this book through. It's not a perfect example of what the Christian life entails - for that, you'd need to read the Bible - but maybe this book will help you understand us a little better. You'll find an appendix at the end which gives you a very simple, no-nonsense explanation about how and why you should receive Christ as your Lord and Savior. You should probably start there and work your way backward.

I hope you enjoy, but, even more, I hope that you learn a great deal about Christianity and that you walk away with a good understanding of what I think it is to live as a Christian.

I hope you learn as much reading this book as I did writing it.

CHAPTER 1:

My Testimony

My testimony is unlike most testimonies that you have heard. I have never done anything very "bad." I have done the typical "wrong" things. I have sinned, as all humans have, but I have not done the very interesting things that become famous.

Despite my "boring" life, I will say, very plainly, that I have lived and died and been brought back a thousand times, and it is in this vein that my thoughts have been colored and shaded. The thoughts that plague a man are affected by his life's experiences and my thoughts are no different.

The man who has lived at ease has no ability to empathize with a man who has lived in sorrow. The man who is unmarried should not offer advice on marriage. That said, I'll try not to speak on things that I know nothing about.

Many Christians have the dubious privilege of saying that Jesus saved them from a life of pornography, drugs, and God only knows what else. It is only by the grace of God, I do not have this testimony. I cannot claim that I am better than anyone else because I do not believe that I am. As Paul expressed, I feel that I am the chief of sinners, for I feel the weight of what I have been redeemed from. That being said, God has sheltered me from some "big sins" for His own purposes and for His glory, and I am forever grateful to Him.

I blame God for my normal life. If only He'd have let me have parents that took their job at parenting a little less seriously or prayed a little less hard, I could have rebelled and gone really off the reservation. However, He gave me parents that took very seriously their charge to raise their only child.

Though there is much to discuss about my early life, for instance, I was raised in a Southern Baptist Church and grew up in a Calvary Chapel, this is not a biography, but a testament of what God has done in my life, through and to me.

Allow me to begin in the 9th grade. I was introduced to high school and all the trials and tribulations that come of puberty in a Christian high school. As with many children who were raised in the church and were exposed to Christians and Christians only, I became very good at being arrogant in my own self-righteousness. So good that one day, towards the end of my freshman year, I prayed that, no matter the consequences, God would let me do great things for His Kingdom and that God would use me more than anyone I knew. I was such a idiot that year. However, God does answer prayers, knowing better than we what our real motives were and knowing, better than we, if what we pray for is a good thing. And God did use me, but it was not the pleasure cruise that I had hoped for.

Therefore, someday shortly after September 11th, 2001, in my sophomore year of high school, God spoke to me in that still, small Voice, telling me to hold signs and open doors. I can't lie; it was a weird thing to be told, and I didn't really want to do it...and I didn't really know what I was supposed to do, but, I began holding signs out by the front doors of my school. I would open a door, hold a sign that had a Christian message, and occasionally pass out a tract with a little inspiring (or convicting) note. My Sophomore year of high school was the first year that I lived my Christianity, and was therefore very difficult and confusing.

I did not have anyone I could turn to in my church for guidance; my youth minister was called to go elsewhere, and I cried bitterly when I heard the news. I gave the new guy a hard time...in fact, I did everything I could to drive him out. Frankly, I was about as unchristian as a person could be towards this man. Of course, looking back, I see that it was the irrational action of a boy trying to hold on to someone he loved, but I will always feel the loss of not getting to know my new youth minister. He could have helped me during my difficult sophomore year, but I didn't let him. In fact, my attitude towards him best reflects the arrogant righteousness that I discussed earlier as I felt that I was better than he was (which, of course, I wasn't).

I did not have a teacher that I felt I could get advice from, because I did not yet know who cared. Some came close, but that year, I was looking for more than a teacher or a friend; I was looking for...help.

I couldn't ask my parents because...well, at that point, my parents were not really sure why I was doing what I was doing. They knew I was a Christian – for they were Christians as well – but they were afraid that I was acting foolishly and with little thought of the consequences of my actions. They were, of course, right, but that has never really stopped me from doing much of anything. Either way, right or wrong, I didn't confide much in my parents, though I now wish I had.

Help did not come, so I retreated into the only two worlds I knew; the world of my own self-imposed spirituality and the world of acting. Oh, how I loved (and still love) acting! It gave me a chance to escape the shell of myself that I was coming to hate and play someone else. Someone "better" or at least someone that was morally redeeming in some way. Or, at last, someone that was not me.

Time wore on, and so did the door-holding ministry. In my junior year of high school, what had been tract-handing, door-holding, and sign-carrying was abandoned as I felt called to lead a prayer group and then a Bible Study. I was not very good at either. I have no idea if God called me to do these things, but I felt that He did as I heard the same small Voice that had told me to open doors. I had four people come to the Bible study and only one person consistently came to the prayer meetings. As it turned out, I was a terrible leader and my prayers seemed to bounce off the sky as nothing seemed to change. I felt like a spiritual failure. Perhaps this was God trying to teach me humility. If that was God's objective, then He succeeded in spades.

The 2002/2003 school year found me hating myself, because I was a smart aleck, always with a witty, if weird, retort for anything any teacher had to say. I would isolate myself from my fellow students with my eccentricities and would judge my peers for being hypocrites. Of course, I knew that I, too, was a hypocrite, and I hated myself all the more for that.

Even worse, I had some sort of weird fainting disease that could not be diagnosed, but would drive me crazy with its frequency. I'd describe this disease more, but, to be honest, I really don't remember that much about it other than it was a shadow of the trials to come. Whether I remember the details or not, I know for certain that what I went through was deliberately planned by God so that I could be prepared for the trials He would send my way in college.

In my senior year (2003/2004), returning from summer vacation, the work of humility that God had begun in me the previous year continued, but this time I allowed God to have His way with me. I determined to do away with all false pretense and focus on what mattered. I went back to opening doors, but I decided this time, the tracts were to be abandoned. All I did was hold a sign that said "Jesus loves you" and held that sign day-after-day, all year long, for 20 minutes before class started. Simplicity seemed to be the way to go.

Of course, that would be the year that the cynic in me grew, as I saw how I had acted previously, I hated the self-righteous zeal that I once had, and began to be cynical about those same traits that I saw in others around me...but that is another story for another time and probably had nothing to do with the signs. The important thing was that I had gotten over my whiny, angsty, self-hating phase. Thank God.

Graduation rapidly approached. My senior year had sped by and I enjoyed every minute of it, spending most of my time making cynical comments in Student Council (ha ha, oh how I loved 4th period Student Council), and would spend all of lunch break playing Hearts with some of my best friends; some of the few friends from high school that would stick with me into college and beyond.

Despite the efforts of several doctors, I was given no clear answers as to what was going on in my body and am STILL awaiting concrete answers.

At my school, the graduating seniors would put on a chapel where they would have a chance to say a few words of wisdom to the rest of the school. For some reason, I was nominated to organize that year's chapel. It was one of the best experiences of my life. I had one of my best friends sing "Who Am I?" by Casting Crowns, I had the Student Body President give a speech about...I think it was something about always trusting God. I'm not entirely sure. And finally, some friends and I did a skit, done to music, which featured me, as Satan, getting knocked around by Jesus, who was played by my best friend. I had gotten tired of seeing some kind of passive Jesus that cried and occasionally helped the sinner. I wanted a manly Jesus (yet another bout of self-righteousness rearing its ugly head). I told my friend not to pull any punches, and he didn't. The school loved watching me get beat up and gave an enthusiastic cheer at the very end. I couldn't have been happier (despite the bruises).

At the end of the chapel, I grabbed a microphone and issued an apology to several people for being a...well, I couldn't actually tell them what I <u>actually</u> thought I was. It was a Christian school, after all.

I told the students in that assembly that the most important thing they would ever hear in their entire lives was that Jesus loved them; just a minor, insignificant detail that was thrown in at the last moment. After speaking for about 45 seconds, I hung up the microphone, and left to thunderous applause. Frankly, I don't care if they remembered a single minute of that hour-long chapel; I just hope those kids remember that Jesus loves them.

After high school, life really soared. I would say that my 18th year of life was the best I have enjoyed thus far. I was in a Christian fraternity where I loved most of the guys; I had a job at Kmart for a good part of that year; and I was...well, I was a terrible engineering student, but I quickly found a degree that better suited me. My love for God abounded and I got to know Him very well. I repeated the prayer I had prayed in high school, about being used greatly by Him, but, having been humbled by Him already, I said something I'll never forget "God, I understand what I am asking for. I understand that when I ask for this, You will allow all kinds of bad things to happen to me so that You may shape me into who You want me to be so that you may use me. Please do." I don't think I was as prepared for Him to answer that prayer as I thought I was.

I continued acting, and did "Hamlet" in the summer and then I did one final play before God allowed life to hit the fan.

"Bullshot Crummond." A cheesy parody-comedy that I still love to reminisce about. During this play, all of the training that God had been preparing me for in high school suddenly became necessary. In the second Act of the play, I lost consciousness for a few seconds and for six months afterward, I walked with a cane because something happened that day that no one could explain, and it messed me up. It felt odd being a 19 year old man, walking around my campus, cobbled to a cane. Many were the night I cried, because I had thought I was ready for the trials to come and I was not.

Of course, the story does not end there. It never does. During those six months, I began to exhibit traits of a disease that I had never heard of and that most doctors hadn't either. One afternoon, I took a nap, because I felt particularly tired. I attempted to roll over, but found that I could not move. Only through extreme effort could I force any muscle to work. I was scared. What began as a type of sleep paralysis expanded into my waking hours. I would be sitting, realize I could not move, but for some reason, at that time, I could still move my head around and talk normally. Except for in extreme circumstances, I could carry on as if nothing happened if I sat still.

In May of 2006, I lost all control. My head slumped down one day and refused to move back up. My arms would not respond to my commands and my legs were frozen in place. I would lose my balance and fall out of chairs or down stairs. Talking came only through great effort, as my lips were all but immobile, though my tongue was flapping like always. If my head was tilted wrong, my flow of oxygen was cut off, so I constantly surrounded myself with people so that if I went paralyzed, they could hold my head so I did not pass out and die. In hindsight, it was not fair that I put the burden of keeping me alive on so many people, but at the time, I wanted to try to live as normal a life as possible, and that included being around my friends, even when I put them in danger.

For almost three years, this went on. The disease struck me often. It would come and go, sometimes three times in a day for an hour a time. I gradually deteriorated to the point where I would start twitching, then thrashing, then doing all manner of bizarre things with this disease. But after May of 2006, I stopped being afraid. I knew that if I died, I was going to be with Jesus. Actually, to be honest, the greatest fear I had did not come from dying, but from having to live on and linger with this disease. Part of me hoped that someone wouldn't be around when it happened, and I could finally be freed.

Many of us hope; several of us assume, but few of us know with certainty that Heaven is coming. During this period of my life, I was so certain that I welcomed the attacks because I felt that they were a step closer to going Home. It wasn't just a desire to be released from pain, although I certainly welcomed that, it was because I had grown very, very close to Jesus during this time to the point where I could depend on none other and wanted to be around no one but Him.

Through it all, through that dark, dismal period, my friends and family stuck close by me. I love them for that. They would help me laugh because, once I began to embrace the possibility of death, the disease stopped being frightening and became hilarious to me because my body would contort into the most bizarre positions, contracting muscles would twist my fingers so that I looked like I was flipping people off, I would spasmodically grasp things, including my own hair or other people nearby; it was so funny, I could hardly stop laughing, and most people, once they got over the initial shock, found that they could laugh right along with me.

In the Spring of 2007, my disease degenerated to the point where I would jerk and twist and turn and wind up injuring myself and others. Eventually, I moved out of my fraternity, because I no longer wanted them to be liable in case I died on their watch...so I moved in with my parents, who were glad that I loved them enough to come home and let them help me.

Not every experience with this disease was bad. In the Spring of 2006 – when I was still using a cane to hobble around – God talked to me in the shower. He put into my mind the door-holding that I had done at my high school and told me to do it again at my university. At this point, I had none of the usual objections: "But God, I'm sick, what if they make fun of me, what if I lose my friends?" I was just ready and willing to get out and do something meaningful again. I was tired of being a sack of potatoes.

And so the door ministry started again. At least three days out of the week, as my schedule would allow, I parked myself at the front doors of the most visited building on campus – the Memorial Union – and would open doors for people, greet them, and hold a sign that said "Jesus loves you." I did this for another three years; until I graduated in the fall of 2008. I have no idea what impact that had on people. I don't know if anyone was permanently changed because of it, or if people just liked looking at the nice – if crazy – redhead that opened doors for people.

I am still surprised at how positive the reaction was from the majority of people. Most people looked at it, smiled, and thanked me for opening the doors for them. Quite a few Christians gave the usual response "Praise God (but please, oh please don't ask me to help)!" There were some unpleasant encounters; some people cussed me out in most creative fashions. One lady was very upset at the audacity of someone promoting one religion over another on a college campus and reported me. Fortunately, I was spared from any unpleasant encounter, once it became obvious to the people in charge that I was not being a pest to people and was not causing a disruption on the campus.

In the years since I first became ill, God has taught me many lessons that I probably could not have learned otherwise; so many that I cannot cover them in one small chapter (hence the entirety of this book). He has taught me grace and forgiveness; mercy and kindness; love and compassion. So many things He has taught me, although so many things I rarely put into practice. Called "being human," I guess.

Of the things I learned, only two lessons are worth mentioning in this chapter and I believe that a man can live his entire life and still not understand these two truths.

First, I learned the importance of laughing with Jesus. God is awe-inspiring and fear is the proper response to the Creator of the Universe. But the Creator of the universe made a monkey and He made a giraffe and He made Man with a sense of humor. I cannot imagine that He does not love to laugh. Sometimes, I was by myself when I was paralyzed, so I cracked jokes with God. He's a great audience but He can be very hard to hear sometimes. Even now in church, during worship, I will find something funny, whisper it to God, and then laugh a bit as I imagine Him laughing along with me. Everyone around me thinks I am crazy, but that's ok; they are just in denial about how crazy they are themselves.

Finally, the most important thing I have learned through living with my disease is that life is equally hard for every human being. The fact that I went through this is gauged on what God knew I could go through. Everyone around me said that it must be so hard to endure what I was going through. I couldn't tell them the truth, because they would not believe it; that what I was going through is probably no harder for me than what they either were going through or would eventually have to endure. It's all a matter of what God wants to happen and when.

This sounds very Calvinistic of me, but it really is not, because God knows what we can handle…but we don't always live up to this potential. We either soar or sink under the stress we are placed under. Enduring through pain and suffering is the only way a Christian can grow. It's written in the Bible on nearly every page. Unfortunately, we have been taught from birth that pain is something to be avoided at all costs. It's an inbred trait that all humans possess.

None of us want to accept that pain is good for us because we want to have something to hate. We want to have a clearly defined enemy that we can loathe and pain provides us with a perfect adversary. However, the Christian ought not to hate pain, but to love it for what it is: God speaking to us.

God speaking to us in such a way that we would be fools to ignore Him. God speaking to us in such a blatant and obvious manner that we cannot help but hear Him, even if we deliberately stop up our ears against Him. Pain is the tool that crafts Christians into the image of Christ. Trials produce perseverance, perseverance produces character, character, hope, and hope does not disappoint because God constantly tells us, through the Holy Spirit, that He loves us.

We are constantly being shaped into the image of Christ, if we allow the Holy Spirit to do this work in us. How? By acknowledging in every hard time – in every failed job, in every disease, in every destroyed relationship, in every death – dear God, may Your holy name be praised, for though I cannot understand what good will come from this, I know that You have promised that some good will come, whether or not that good is directly for me, I know Your name will be glorified.

And that is what it is all about: God's name being glorified. Everything else is just gravy.

I pray that God would be so merc5iful to everyone reading this or hearing this to give them a trial in their lives that would do three things:

- Make the person dependent on God
- Make them want to know Him better
- Make them constantly aware that this earth is not our home

Job summed it up neatly, and this has been my favorite verse for years:

"For I know that my Redeemer lives, and He shall stand at last on the Earth. And after my skin is destroyed, this I know, that in my flesh, I shall see God. Whom I shall see for myself, and my eyes shall behold, and not another. How my heart yearns within me!"

How my heart yearns within me! Oh, Jesus, come soon. Please, please. Come soon. Or, barring that, take me home when You are finished with me. When I have done all that You ask of me. When my mission is complete and when Your name has been glorified through my life. For this land is not my home, but is a testing ground, and I long to pass this test and finally, finally see Your face and hear Your voice and to laugh, at last, with You.

This, then, is the introduction to the book you are about to read. You needed to hear from the donkey's mouth all that I have gone through, because only then will you understand that my qualifications to write this book about Christianity come not from any divinity doctorate, or through the masses that I have led to Christ, or because I preach to a church that boasts a congregation larger than a small city, but simply because I am a man of God who loves Him very much, and desires to know Him more. True, I may be young, but, as Paul admonished Timothy, I ought not be looked down upon because I am young. God uses the poor and unlikely things in the world to put to shame the wise people; the doctorates; the MENSA Men and what is more poor and unlikely than some kid who just got out of college?

I hope you enjoy reading this as much as I have enjoyed writing it.

CHAPTER 2:

The Early Fundamentals

Every sports coach knows that the most important thing for his players to know are the basic fundamentals of the game. I'm sure that those of you who played sports in high school or college remember the grizzled coach, disappointed in the hot-shot antics of his team, saying in that no-nonsense voice, "Alright, boys, we got sloppy, so now we gotta get back to fundamentals. Give me fifty wind sprints and the first person to complain does another twenty."

We all know that there is more to any sport, job, or activity than the fundamental elements, but we all need to know the basics before we can learn the more advanced stuff. The same is true with Christianity.

The author of Hebrews, you know, "what's-his-name," wrote a scathing indictment against the Jewish Christians, about how they were at the point in their walks when they should have been teaching others, but were instead so immature that they still needed to be taught the basics.

Going back to the sports metaphor, the audience of Hebrews were supposed to be making diving catches and executing perfect hit-and-run maneuvers, but they were still stuck learning how to hold the bat and figuring out how to throw the ball.

We see in today's church a similar trend that the early Christians had when it comes to only knowing the basics and nothing else. We have our "Sunday-only Christians" that come to church, might read an inspirational book or read about how their lives need to have more "purpose," or how they can pray a special prayer and, magically, everything wrong with their lives will fall into place and then think they have fulfilled their requirements for being a Christian.

These people don't "know" God in the Father-son relationship that the Bible says that He wants to cultivate.

Well, the purpose of this chapter isn't about harping on immature Christians (there are other chapters for that), but is rather about laying down a foundation for this book by briefly covering the fundamentals of Christianity that the Hebrews-author (we'll just call him "Paul," because it saves space and because I think the book's author was Apostle Paul) had refused to talk on.

I am, of course, not placing myself above Paul, because he knew the audience to whom he was writing, whereas I do not. I have no idea where you are on the spectrum of Christian learning, so we will have a brief refresher course in the basics.

In his accusation to the Jewish Christians, Paul lists the fundamental teachings of Christianity: repentance from dead works, faith towards God, baptisms, laying on of hands, and resurrection of the dead and eternal judgment. I'll briefly cover each of these in this chapter, except for faith, because I cover that in the next chapter.

Repentance from dead works

The Bible says that all of our good works are as dirty rags before God. I have heard two different definitions for what is implied by "dirty rags." One implies a cloth that a leper would wrap around his wounds to keep others from seeing him. These cloths were ritually unclean, they stunk of dead flesh, and they had touched leprosy, which is a generic term for any kind of skin disease that rotted the flesh and destroyed the nerves. The Bible uses leprosy as an allegory for sin.

Much like leprosy, sin destroys the "nerves" of our conscience. The first time we sin we usually know that what we are doing is wrong. Shooting up heroin? We know it's wrong. Having sex with our secretary? Totally wrong. Cheating on our taxes? Well, Jesus said to give to Caesar what is Caesar's and to God what is God's, so even cheating on our taxes is a sin. Every time we sin, it becomes easier to sin the next time. It's like drinking alcohol. The first time, you may hate the taste. Depending on how much you drank, you may cough for a while and possibly puke. People say that alcohol is an "acquired taste," so you build up immunity to the coughing and start to enjoy the taste and appreciate the feeling of being drunk. Sinning, then, is like alcohol, except for the fact that a person does not have to acquire a taste for sinning. We all do it; we all like it. Therefore, perhaps a more accurate analogy would be to compare sinning to eating peanuts; you cannot stop with just one peanut, and you cannot stop sinning.

Therefore, to say that a person's good deeds are like a leper's rags is like putting makeup on a pig. You are trying to cover up your sins, but you are not succeeding. Even if you're fooling everyone around you, you cannot hide sin from God and God isn't fooled.

The second interpretation for "filthy rags" that I have heard is that they are likened to menstrual rags. They didn't have tampons back in the day, so women had to stop their bleeding with strips of cloth. I imagine it was very unpleasant back in the day.

In the Mosaic Law, a woman going through her period was ceremonially unclean and could not worship in the temple.

These rags were a testament to this uncleanliness and that woman's inability to worship God. Our sin-covered "good deeds" are like menstrual rags because our good deeds are not good enough to bring us into the presence of a holy God. If we try to barter our way in with how "good" we think we are, then our good works are proof, not that we deserve to be saved, but that we are unclean before God and cannot worship Him in our present state.

Whichever definition you prefer – covering a deadly disease (which cannot be covered) or proving a person's incapability to worship God – it should be stated plainly that our good works are dead before God and cannot possibly please Him. Enter Jesus.

Most of you who are reading this book will know that Jesus was/is God-who-became-Man who lived among us for 33 years. He showed us that our methods to reach holiness, which we thought were working, weren't and showed us that the true path to God the Father was through Him. For claiming to be God (and because they were jealous of His popularity), the Pharisees brought Jesus to the Romans, who eventually executed Him for – get this – being who He claimed He was. Even in the crucifixion of Jesus, we can find some irony that we will probably laugh about in Heaven.

However, His death was not a tragic mistake, but a calculated plan to make it possible for the sins of all mankind to be forgiven. On the cross, as Jesus was dying, all the sins that humanity had committed or would ever commit were heaped upon Him and his death paid the penalty for all those sins.

You see, when God first gave the Law to Moses, He made it clear that innocent blood had to be shed on behalf of the guilty so that the punishment that rightly belonged to the guilty party would be transferred to the innocent. At that time, the innocent sacrifice was a lamb; an imperfect sacrifice, because the lamb could not choose to be perfect. Only when God became Man could the sacrifice of the Innocent for the guilty be made complete.

When we receive Jesus' gift of salvation, we are repenting of our efforts to make ourselves better; to make ourselves like unto God (which was mankind's first sin as recorded in Genesis), and we are requesting that Jesus become our Lord, our Master. As I read the Bible, "repentance from dead works" is the forgiveness of sin and the bringing to life of the spirit that comes about when Jesus works on a person.

Baptisms

Anytime one Christian points to one verse about baptism, some other Christian points to another verse that seems to contradict the first view and I don't know why there must be a confusion among us. Some people say that baptism is necessary for you to go to Heaven; some say that baptism is completely unnecessary and extraneous; others say that baptism is an outward symbol for an inward change. Of course, there are other views, but these three views are the most common and should be covered, lest we leave unspoken something important.

The first perspective, which states that you need to be baptized to be saved, adds an additional requirement to salvation. Jesus + X = salvation, if you will. The Bible includes dozens of verses that clearly state that belief is all that is necessary for salvation (Ephesians 2:8-9, Romans 10, etc), but there are a few verses that can be taken to mean that salvation and baptism go hand-in-hand to save a person. For instance, Jesus' last command to the Christians was that they go into the entire world, make disciples, and baptize them. In another place, Peter says you must be saved and baptized. These verses, taken by themselves, can lead a person into confusion and error.

Since we have verses from both sides of the argument, let's take things in context without just drawing from single verses. In fact, let's use an example. As Jesus was dying on the cross, a thief on one side of Him (traditionally, the thief on His right side) pleaded to Jesus that He remember him when He came into His kingdom. This thief, who might have heard of Jesus but was probably not well versed in His doctrine, had made a decision that Jesus had to have been who He said He was and so the thief, in his last few moments on earth, cries out to Jesus and Jesus said to Him, "Today you will be with Me in Paradise." In other words, without being baptized, Jesus declared this man saved.

A person could claim that this was an exceptional case and only applied once for one man. Ok. In that case, you are making the Gospel less about grace and more about works. You are saying that it is "grace + baptism = Heaven." Seriously? I was baptized when I was 21 in the summer of 2008. I had been saved long before that point because I could feel the Holy Spirit inside of me, having talked to Him on occasion. If a person is not saved until they are baptized, then, despite my love for God, despite my efforts to serve Him, I would have still gone to Hell if I died before the summer of '08 since I had not yet been baptized. I refuse to accept that because there are some things that I do not need proven to me and the fact that I am saved is one of them.

The second opinion about baptism, which says that baptism is unnecessary is equally problematic because it ignores the words of Jesus, the actions of the apostles, and the words of the New Testament writers. Jesus told people to be baptized, the apostles baptized people after those people were saved, and Paul later endorsed baptism.

As I read the Bible, technically you don't have to be baptized. However, Jesus was baptized to give us an example of a ritual that we should observe in our own lives. He was baptized to show us that it is important that we allow ourselves to symbolically say that the old man is dead, represented by being held under the water, and then the new man, brought to life, is alive for Christ and not themselves, as represented by being brought back up from the water. It certainly is not necessary for salvation and a Christian can lead an obedient life without obeying this one command. This leads to the third view, which I personally endorse.

I believe that baptism is a way for a Christian to understand and relate to the death and resurrection of Jesus and the accepting of the New Life that he has been born into. Baptism is a symbol. As a person goes into the water, they are symbolizing that they have died to themselves and their sin and as they emerge from the water, they are stating that they are now living a new life in Christ. It is a witness to fellow Christians, to heathens, and is an Ebenezer; a stone of remembrance (1 Sam 7:12) for the person being baptized and it shows that the person is ready, willing, and able to serve God in the capacity that He determines.

Jesus told us to be baptized and allowed Himself to be baptized as an example to us. Anytime Jesus undergoes something and then tells us to emulate Him, we should consider it of great importance for us to follow His example.

Laying on of hands

I'm not going to lie to ya, this fundamental was really hard for me to interpret. Therefore, I appealed to several commentaries (and a pastor or two) to find a view that made sense, spliced some of their ideas and added some of my own. What did I learn through this cross-referencing? That no two pastors agree on much of anything. I suppose that's the nature of the Bible: much is left open to interpretation so that men may think about the things of God and ponder who He is, although there is certainly, somewhere, a right understanding of what the author was trying to convey.

I have no solid answers for this quandary. The Bible describes people laying their hands on things in different occasions. Believers would lay hands on people they would pray for or try to heal or on people who wanted to be empowered by the Holy Spirit. Therefore, I suppose the common element is that in all three occasions, the Holy Spirit is active, so let us assume that Paul (Hebrews' author, remember) is saying that he is assuming that the people he is writing to have been thoroughly informed about the Holy Spirit and His ministry.

I'm gonna have to be really brief about this, because people have written large tomes about the Holy Spirit. He is just that interesting a character and He is the only one of the Trinity that we do not seem to understand. God the Father makes sense to us: He is the authority figure that controls all. God the Son makes sense to us: When God the Father wants something, God the Son gets it done. The Holy Spirit, however, is harder for us modern Christians to understand.

We in America live in a society that swings on a pendulum of extremes: we either do not believe in the spiritual side of things or we have weird beliefs about spirituality. Many of us live very scientific lives that assert that there is no room for unexplainable phenomena and that there is no such thing as an invisible, personable Spirit who dwells inside of Christians and who talks – in a lesser degree – to nonbelievers. This dependence on science is in and of itself a religion, but very few men who worship at the altar of Newton, Einstein, and Bohr would dare admit that they are high priests to a very depressing and impersonal god.

Even we Christians have odd beliefs about the Holy Spirit, either ignoring Him, or exalting Him and His ministry to a level that is, quite frankly, unhealthy. So who is the Holy Spirit? To be honest, I'm not entirely sure. I've read an awful lot of books that describe who He is, but it does not make sense to me, so I will try to explain the Holy Spirit to you through the paradigm that I have come to accept.

When we look at the life and ministry of Jesus, we see that He spent hours in prayer with His Father. Jesus constantly talks about God the Father, but very rarely does He discuss the Holy Spirit, and then only at the end of His life. Jesus told His disciples that He would not leave them orphaned when He ascended to Heaven (a concept that they didn't really understand), but that His departure would usher in the Holy Spirit, Who would remain with the disciples (and by extension, all Christians) forever.

In other words, we see the purposes of the Father, Son, and Spirit in this segment, I do believe. We see the Father, whose presence is infinite (Psalm 139), we see the Son, who has a glorified body that, though it is more than human (Heb 2:9) is still confined to a specific point in time (John 20: 19-29), and we see the Holy Spirit, Who, like the Father, is not restricted by space and lives in the hearts of all believers (John 14:17)

Like the Son, the Spirit's role is to bring glory to the Father (John 13:31,32, John 16:13, 14). And like the Father, the Spirit's role is to glorify the Son (see the same two passages). Yes, the mystery of the God, three personalities, but one God, is enough to boggle the mind and, I'm sure if you strain hard enough to think on it, you'll cause a nosebleed.

For we know that each of the members of the Trinity have a distinct personality and can inhabit the same space in time as three separate entities, as evidenced by the baptism of Jesus, where Jesus, in human form, had the Spirit come down from Heaven, while the Father was speaking.

We have no problem believing that the Father is a person and that the Son is a person, but we often forget that the Holy Spirit is a person as well, for there is NEVER a non-specific pronoun (such as "it") used to refer to the Holy Spirit. He is always called "He." This is not an issue about whether or not the Spirit of God is male of female, for the Holy Spirit is not a flesh-and-blood man to whom gender applies. Instead, like God the Father, the Holy Spirit is given a masculine pronoun because we associate authority and power with males.

As discussed in the *Handbook of Christian Apologetics*, by Peter Kreeft and Robert Tracelli, if God were to call Himself by the feminine pronouns, it would imply that A) the universe was birthed - as was the case in the Creation-myths in the pagan religions - rather than externally created, and B) by the same token, there was to be no confusion that God externally works to save the soul rather than we ourselves being the power behind our own salvation (Kreeft, Tracelli, pg 98).

Sorry, went off on a bit of a tangent with the "Holy Spirit's gender" issue, but I didn't want the question to go unanswered, and I didn't think it needed an entire chapter in a book that is not an apologetic for who God is.

Back to the Holy Spirit. So, we know that He is a person because He is given attributes that are only used to describe a person. For instance, we know that the Holy Spirit can be grieved when we act as though we weren't saved (Eph 4:25-31). By the same token, we can infer that the Holy Spirit can be pleased when we act in a manner befitting Christians, by being kind to one another, by showing mercy, and forgiving each other (Eph 4:32).

So that's who I believe the Holy Spirit is. He is the One who lives inside of us, the conscience that tells us to avoid certain things and to pursue others. It is He that convicts the World of sin (John 16:8). It is He that allows us Christians to have the courage to stand before people and talk boldly about Christ Jesus (Acts 2:33).

The Bible tells us that the Spirit encourages us with the constant reminder that we are sons of God. The Holy Spirit seems to communicate with God on our behest when we don't know what we're supposed to be saying in our prayers. This is a great mercy because I know that I myself rarely know what I am supposed to say in any given circumstance.

For this reason, I believe the Bible describes the Holy Spirit's ministry as one of pointing people to Christ, who leads people to the Father. When we do not notice the Holy Spirit's working, I do not think He minds as long as we pay due respect to the Father.

So that's who He is, according to my limited understanding. You should research Him yourself and find out more than I can write in these scant few pages, because the Holy Spirit is a really interesting Person.

Resurrection of the Dead

I imagine that Paul was referring to the heresy of the Sadducees which stated that there is no resurrection from the dead; you die and that's it. Oblivion. Since this was a heresy that was devised by Jewish leaders (granted, the idea of the no resurrection from the dead was not limited to the Sadducees) and since the book of Hebrews was written to Jews, I believe that Paul included this as a "fundamental" because he wanted his readers to accept as rote the fact that, at some point in time, Jesus was going to raise the dead; the nonbelievers to everlasting damnation and the believers to everlasting bliss. I'll explain why resurrection is so important later on.

It is interesting that Christians still believe that "you live, you die, that's all, folks," even after Jesus had a showdown with the Sadducees right before He was crucified. In rapid succession, Jesus was asked some final questions by his biggest enemies, the Pharisees, the Sadducees, and the lawyers or scribes. The Sadducees asked Jesus a hypothetical question.

Let's say we have a man, we'll call him "Jerry." Jerry takes a wife, Betty, but Jerry dies before he can get Betty pregnant. Under Moses' Law, Betty must marry Jerry's brother, have a baby, and thus preserve Jerry's name. Unfortunately, in this scenario, Jerry's brother dies before he can get Betty pregnant, and this goes on down the line for all of Jerry's family until they are all dead. Betty was obviously a very scary person to marry. Finally, Betty dies (and stops killing every man that touches her) and goes to Heaven, where all her impotent husbands are waiting. The Sadducees then asked Jesus which of the men would be considered Betty's husband in Heaven?

They were trying to catch Jesus on a technicality because they did not believe that the dead would ever see the light of day again. In their eyes, resurrection from the dead was simply not possible since it was not talked about much in the Old Testament (although, the Sadducees apparently ignored the book of Job, where Job constantly talks about a physical resurrection from the dead).

Jesus, as was His fashion, not only answered the question they asked, but also went deeper, into the heart of the matter, to expose the fallacy of their beliefs. He said that the dead are not going to be given in marriage to one another, so no one would get the woman and the woman would get no one. He went on to criticize the Sadducees, for they knew the Law and what we Christians call the Old Testament, but they had neglected to remember the passage that is echoed throughout the Old Testament. God is the God of Abraham, Isaac, and Jacob. Not He "was" the God of these men, but He "is" currently, presently, and continuously. Meaning these men have not disappeared into oblivion as the Sadducees would have wanted.

Even more important for us the Christian, if the soul lives on after death, then the resurrections that Jesus performed and His own resurrection from the dead become possible. If the soul does die, then Jesus could not have brought people back and He would have stayed in the grave because His soul would have vanished into nothingness. There would be nothing to resurrect and if He did come back, He would come back a zombie.

Therefore, if you are a Christian, Paul is saying that you should believe that you will go to Heaven, and that your soul will live on after death. Otherwise, what is the point of being a Christian if there is no afterlife, no Heaven ? If there is no reward; if there is no permanent dwelling place with Christ, then Christ was either a liar when He said that He would prepare a place for us in Heaven, or He was making promises that He could not fulfill and was giving us false hope. Not only that, but Paul goes on to say in 1st Corinthians 15:16-19 that if Christ did not raise from the dead, then we are still dead in our sins, and if we have only have this life, then we Christians are the most pitiable of all men. If either of these are true, then our faith is invalid and Christianity falls apart. Therefore, we Christians have to accept, on faith, that there is a resurrection from the dead for us because, outside of the Bible, we have no proof, unless we are among the lucky few that have seen a person brought back from death.

Faith leaves men in very difficult positions sometimes. It forces us to believe something on limited evidence; it forces us to make a logical leap from the evidence that we have to a conclusion that may or may not be true. The Christian, though, is not a man prone to blind leaps of faith, but one who reasons out his faith with fear and trembling. We believe that there is a resurrection from the dead, first because the Bible tells us so, but also because the Holy Spirit who lives within us constantly speaks to us, putting eternity into our minds, so that we do not forget the hope that is Heaven and the reality that is the immortal soul.

Eternal Judgment

The inevitability of judgment is a very unpopular part of Christianity that none of us have wanted to honestly believe in. Even in the Middle Ages, when Hell and eternity were used to scare the peasantry into line, no one believed in eternal judgment, or else they would have lived differently.

Today's pastor fears to talk about judgment, either the kind that affects the believer or the nonbeliever. Such talk rocks the boat; it hurts feelings; it causes guilt. In our sugar-coated Christian world, nothing is more destructive than the truth that there is an accounting for whether we have received Christ and for what we have done with our lives. Therefore, we have excised this vital truth from our minds and have tried to forget that there will one day be an accounting for everything that we have ever thought or done.

The word "Hell" gets tossed around a lot in today's society. Very few people acknowledge it as a real place and most of those that do believe in it believe that it will be the final resting place for only the truly wicked (Hitler, Stalin, etc). Many think of "Hell" as a curse word rather than as the final resting place of the damned. As is often the case, the Bible teaches something different from the sensibilities of modern culture.

When people think of Hell's place in the Bible, we tend to think of the Old Testament, for we think there is a difference between the God that is in the Old Testament and the God of the New Testament. We tend to believe that God was harsh, cruel, and unnecessarily strict in the Old Testament, but that He mellowed out a bit in the New Testament. We think, maybe He matured and grew up or perhaps He started taking some cosmic valium. Oddly enough, most of the information we have about Hell comes from the teachings of Jesus rather than from passages in the Old Testament.

Jesus talked about Hell an awful lot, not so much to scare us into Heaven, but to warn us away. For instance, let's say your name's Joe and you're walking alone in the Arizona desert. You are a smart fellow because you thought to bring some water and SPF 35. However, nobody warned you about rattlesnakes.

As you are walking along, you happen to see a snake sunbathing. You think that this snake is the most fascinating thing you have ever seen, so you reach down to pet him. Sammy the Snake does not like being touched, so he bites you. Sammy is a hemotoxic snake, so when he bites you, your blood cells start to burst, your organs start to disintegrate, and your skin starts to slough off you. You die an agonizingly painful death while Sammy the Snake continues his little sunbathing.

See, if you had been told about rattlesnakes, there is a chance that you would not have touched Sammy. Of course, if you knew about snakes and STILL touched Sammy, then you are very stupid.

Well, let's say that God is like the friendly park ranger that warns you against touching rattlesnakes. Like the ranger talking about the dangers of snakes, God tells you about Hell, explaining the peril of going there and goes into graphic detail so that you have been told about how terrifying Hell is.

When God talks about Hell, He uses very colorful word pictures. Hell is described as the outer darkness, a place of torment, a place of fire, but a place where there is no death, only torment. It is the only place in Creation that God will not allow His presence to be felt because the citizens of Hell have decided that they do not want God to reign over them...so He doesn't.

Different words in the Bible describe different realms of Hell. The Hebrew word *Sheol*, translated *Hades* in Greek, refers to a holding cell for people who died. It's like an eternal waiting room where the damned will be consciously aware of what is happening. As we learn from Jesus' parable of the Rich Man and Lazarus, Hades was at one point separated into a section for the righteous and the unrighteous.

The righteous would stay in a place called "Abraham's Bosom" and the damned would be separated by an impassable rift and would stay in torment, bemoaning their unrighteous living. When Jesus died, we read that He set prisoners free, which some take to mean that He took the people from Abraham's Bosom up to the intermediate Heaven, where they could dwell in the presence of God. The people in the bad side of Hades stayed where they were to await the final judgment.

Hell itself is called "Gehenna." This is the big one; the scariest word that the Bible uses because of what it meant historically. In ancient Israel, there was a valley known as Hinnom. It lay near Jerusalem and was a place for idol worship. In this valley, great idols to the god Molech would be erected. The idols would be heated until they glowed red with heat and then petitioners of the god would place their still-living infants into the red-hot arms of the demon-god. In later years, the valley of Hinnom would be a garbage dump and a place to burn the bodies of criminals. It was stinky, constantly on fire, and always smoking. Gehenna refers to the final judgment, the place where the unrepentant spend eternity.

Think of Hades and Sheol as the holding cells for the unrepentant sinners and Gehenna as the maximum security prison that they eventually get transferred to.

Jesus once said that in the final judgment, there will be people that will cry out "Lord, Lord, have we not prophesied in Your name, cast out demons in Your name, and done many wonders in Your name?" Jesus' answer is terrifying: "I never knew you; depart from Me, you who practice lawlessness."

In this passage, Jesus had been discussing hypocrisy and false teachers, saying that those who were false would bear bad fruit (actions and teachings). In other words, many pastors, many religious leaders of many different denominations will come before the throne of judgment, only to have their application for Heaven shredded as they hear the words, "I never knew you. You never took the time to know Me, despite My best efforts. You have no right to be here. Get out of My sight."

Hell is a terrifying prospect because the very thought of it should make every Christian ensure that he really does know God. That he really has asked for forgiveness, made Christ the Master of his life, and has endeavored to know Him through His Word. I am not adding anything to the Gospel by saying this, for the Bible clearly states that if you call out on the name of the Lord, you shall be saved, but I am saying that you need to make sure that you made a serious commitment rather than a decision that was based on an emotional high.

Who will be in Hell? Paul gives a list of sins in 1st Corinthians 6:9-11 which essentially boils down to this: sinners will be in Hell. People who have decided that they would rather live their lives as they wanted rather than as God wanted them to. People that did not yield control of their lives to God but instead insisted on flying the plane of their life...straight into the ground. Basically, anybody you know could be in Hell, and since we have all rebelled against God, we all deserve to go there.

Hell is real, guys, because sin cannot stand in the presence of a just and holy God. It shrinks in terror; it recoils in fear; it grimaces in agony. Sin cannot abide to be near God because sin is the antithesis of God. It is in direct contradiction to His nature as sin is nothing more than a rebellion against God. God had to create Hell, but He created it for the demons that fell from Heaven. It was never intended for Man. Man, however, was stubborn. He insisted that he wanted his own way, so God let him have his way. If a person will not accept God's gift of salvation, then God will not force a person into Heaven. They have chosen Hell and they must accept the consequences of this decision. And so must the rest of us.

We Christians have been given a mission to seek out the lost. It is not our duty to save people from Hell for only the Holy Spirit can do that. It is our job to show the unbelievers who Jesus really is, explain to them the stakes that lay before them, and pray that they make the right decision. And, by God's grace, some may be saved. Pray for your friends and family, for Hell is no joke and it is no fantasy. It is a reality, albeit one we cannot yet see.

Now, judgment is not just for the nonbeliever. Paul describes a time when every work that a Christian does, be it good or bad, will be measured and God will "melt away" – forget – all of the deeds we have done that were not done for His glory and will reward us for the good that we did in His Name. Jesus talked about such a time as well when He said that every man would be judged according to his deeds. For the unbeliever, whose deeds are as filthy rags, their deeds can never be good enough. For the believer, who was not saved by their deeds, but through the grace of God, their deeds will be measured and weighed.

I think it very likely that, when it comes to the final judgment, we will more than likely be more surprised at how many good deeds God remembers and how many bad deeds that He forgets.

Allow me to explain. I have heard it said through most of my life that we need to make sure our motives are pure and only that will please God. To suggest this is to suggest something that I think is beyond our capacity as humans. I do not believe any human being can ever act completely altruistically. No matter how small, I think there is always some selfish motivation. Even for the Christian sacrificing his life, he does so because he knows that he is commanded to and that his actions will have consequences that echo across eternity. Even in selflessness, there is human imperfection.

We're human. We're fallen. To act in divine perfection, we first need to be divine, and none of us are. But I believe that God is gracious. I do not believe that He will throw out the baby with the bathwater. I believe that God will sift through the selfish motivations and find the part of us that acted to please Him. The part where our spirit said "God, I do this out of worship for you."

It doesn't have to be something big, it doesn't have to be something done to catch God's attention, because Jesus said that even if someone were to give a child a glass of cold water in the name of a disciple, he would not lose his reward. Bear in mind, Jesus did not say "In My Name." That's how merciful He is. Even if we do the right thing, but our motives are not perfect, He is gracious.

One of my favorite pastors, Jon Coursen, describes the gifts of God in this way: when we were toddlers, all it took to please us was to bang some pots together. Now that we are older, our capacity for enjoyment has increased dramatically and we look at the child banging the pans and realize that we could never be as happy as he is doing the same activity.

In the same way, when we get to Heaven, some people are going to be "banging pots," figuratively speaking, because they did not receive much reward for their lives on earth. They'll still be happy and overjoyed at being in Heaven, but their capacity for enjoyment will not be very great.

By the same token, some people will be flying jet planes (also figuratively speaking) because they dedicated themselves solely to Christ and are able to experience so much more of Heaven than the pot-bangers.

In the last chapter of the book of Revelation, we see Jesus telling us Christians that He is coming soon and that He is bringing His reward with Him to give to each man his due. It would be against His personality to tell us this and then mean for the prospect to terrify us or to frighten us into working harder. There is a popular misconception out there today that goes: "Jesus is coming; look busy."

If you are a Christian, you have no need to fear the return of Jesus, but should rather pray for it daily, not only so that we may get our rewards, but so that we may receive our ultimate Reward: eternity with Jesus.

Thus ends the fundamentals. From here on out, this book talks about the building blocks to make up what is – in my mind – a good Christian. As always, you have the right to disagree, but if you do, provide a basis for it biblically and logically, and always check my statements against your Bible. If I am wrong, I do not want to lead any of you astray, but rather receive a hundred letters from people telling me what I got wrong and why so that I may learn.

CHAPTER 3:

Faith Like a Child

"But without faith it is impossible to please Him, for he who comes to God must believe that He is, and that He is a rewarder of those who diligently seek Him."

Hebrews, chapter 11, verse 6

"...Assuredly, I say to you, unless you are converted and become as little children, you will by no means enter the kingdom of Heaven."

Matthew, chapter 18, verse 3

Faith is a funny thing. In our society, we assume that the only kind of "faith" that a person can have is "blind faith"; the faith of champagne wishes and caviar dreams. This worldview states that people that have faith in something outside of themselves are akin to those that believe in Santa Clause. Taking this a step further, our world believes that if you have faith that Jesus is who He said He was (Son of God, God made incarnate in flesh, only way to God, etc, etc, etc...), then you are most likely a lunatic, on par with someone who runs around naked because they believe that the CIA has bugged their clothing, or someone that thinks that "The X-Files" was actually based on true stories from the FBI.

The problem with our understanding of faith is that we don't realize just how often it is that we exhibit faith. I went to Scotland this September and to get to Scotland, I had three options: travel by plane, travel by boat, swim. I have never really learned how to swim and I hate boats, so that left me with only one option. I had to fly.

Aerodynamics is a funny thing. Something I don't fully understand and am perfectly willing to call "magic." However, supposedly there is some sort of science involved (don't believe it!!!), and as there are some theories floating around that prove that flying is not magic, I thought it worth going to howstuffworks.com to figure out how a plane flies.

An airplane uses massive jet engines to create thrust. This thrust propels the airplane down the runway in an attempt to overcome drag, which is a combination of gravity and friction. If the thrust overcomes drag, then the plane can takeoff. Once the plane gathers enough speed, it uses the wings and tail fins to take advantage of the fact that air is fluid and lifts the plane into the air.

As I read back over the last paragraph, I have no idea what any of this means. I have to accept, by faith, that men smarter than I am have built my airplane in such a way that, somehow, it will fly. I have to rest comfortably in the fact that the overwhelming odds state that I will most likely not crash and die in the plane in which I am traveling.

This is but one, incredibly complicated example of how faith works in our daily lives. As you drive your car, you exhibit faith that your wheels will not fly off the rims and you go careening into a gas-tanker, blowing yourself and dozens of other drivers into smithereens. You exhibit faith every time you open a door, trusting that the hinges will work and the door will not fall on your head. You exhibit faith when you sit in a chair, knowing that the chair was manufactured in a third-world country, which is quite possibly the safest place for a chair to be made, since third-world products have a long history of reliability and safety.

Ergo, let it suffice to say that, for our purposes, faith is the reasoned belief you have that something will happen the way you expect it to. However, the catch-22 is that we never can prove 100%

without a shadow of a doubt that something will work the way we expect it to until we take a leap of faith. In Christianity, we are told to have faith that God will fulfill His promises to us, specifically, salvation. We are asked to believe, first of all, that God exists and we are then asked to believe that He (God) will reward those who seek Him (Heb. 6:11). This is a simple concept with a complex meaning.

That God Exists

We are told to believe God exists. If we assume that faith is a reasonable assumption that things are the way we think they are and that something will occur in the manner in which we expect it to, then there must be some logical, thinking reason for us to believe in God.

There have been dozens of books written by very smart men and women (many of whom are scientists) that chronicle how life did not happen by accident. That some Being (read: God) had to create it because, mathematically, everything that exists in this timeframe had to have a beginning. Therefore, for time itself to exist, an event had to occur to begin time and something outside of the bounds of time had to create time. That being is God. Now, this is simply a theistic argument for proving that life had to spawn from something, and that the processes had to be put into motion by an uncreated Creator. This argument does not necessarily hinge on the Christian God, Yahweh. However, you and I know that I am not talking about Allah, or anyone else, so the theistic argument might as well be a Christian argument in our case.

Logic led us in the previous paragraph and faith must lead us in this paragraph. We believe that something or someone had to create everything that our eyes can see and many that they can't. If someone created this, we are led to believe that that someone had to be uncreated, for there cannot be an unending set of beginnings. Something had to start the ball rolling. That something/someone is God; the Ancient of Days who, we assume, is outside of the time-space continuum, since the Bible makes numerous references to Him not growing old, etc.

Now, frankly, I don't have to prove that God existed to you. If you are reading this, then I am assuming you are a Christian that already believes in the existence of God. If you are looking for a book on apologetics to explain to your friends (and to yourself) why God is real and atheism is invalid, then look somewhere else, because I cannot help you, because that is *not what this book is about*. I'd try several books by Josh McDowell or by J.P. Moreland. These men know what they are talking about, and I will not insult their books by summarizing years of research into a few paragraphs.

Therefore, for the sake of this book, we take for granted that God exists. To please God, you have to believe that He exists. This is like saying that if I am going to go to all the trouble of preparing a very nice meal for a very attractive lady, then I would not be pleased if she looked at the guy standing next to me and assumed that he made that meal for her. Likewise, God is not pleased when He blesses people with health, family, friends, and – you know – existence, and then that person looks at Charles Darwin and says, "Thanks, Chuck! This was really swell of you!"

The next bit requires some careful thought: That He will reward those who seek Him. The Bible promises great things to those that seek God. First of all, Jesus promises that anyone who diligently and persistently seeks will find what they are looking for. I believe that Jesus was implicitly referring to God. In other words, anyone who constantly seeks God will find Him. See the word "constantly?" The author of Hebrews did not say "anyone who feels like seeking God on a Sunday from 10 AM – noon and who then decides to live as a heathen, will be rewarded for those two hours that he sort of gave to God, even though the fellow was really thinking about Sunday Night Football." No, the Greek implies that we are to constantly seek God. Continuously. Fervently. Ardently.

Now, I have heard a lot of different ideas about what it means for God to be a rewarder of those that diligently seek Him. Most of these ideas are complicated and involve some speculation about Heaven. I think, however, that the reward that is talked about here is His company. Think about it: God rewards those that diligently pursue Him; those that take the time to get to know God. I think, therefore, that His reward is that He will be found by those that seek Him. I wish I could offer you an earth-shattering revelation that veritably reeks of newness, but all I can suggest is something that is simple and old: God will be found by those that try to find Him.

We also should look at the manner of faith in which we are supposed to have. All too often we say, "I believe, but [insert qualifying phrase here]." It doesn't matter what we use to fill in that blank, we find some excuse to say to God that we would do what He wants, but we have something better to do or, if we are really honest with ourselves, we don't really believe as we should. I think Jesus makes it very clear to us that this kind of faith is, at the very least, disappointing to Him, and at the very most, could keep a person out of Heaven.

Why do I say this? Well, Jesus said that to enter the Kingdom of Heaven, one must first be converted and become like a child. I don't believe that conversion and becoming like a child are two separate things. I think Jesus is telling us how we become converted: make ourselves like children.

What does it mean, then, to make yourself like a child? Well, that's a good question. Everyone always talks about "childlike innocence," and that seems to be a pretty good description of what "childlike faith" is like. Kids accept things to be true more readily and with greater enthusiasm than us "old folks." Kids are not cynical like we are. They have innocence about them that most of us envy as we see the unhappiness that our doubt, suspicions, fear, and "wisdom" have caused in us.

Therefore, to become like a child, we must set aside our cynicism, release our anger, drop our suspicions, forget our "wisdom," and let go of our fears, and embrace the Gospel of Christ. For instance, let's assume that you are 8-years-old. You and your best friend are playing stickball in the street. You are at bat and your friend is getting ready to pitch to you. All of a sudden, from behind you, you hear the tell-tale music of…the ice cream man. You cannot see the ice cream man, but your friend can, and he's running straight towards him screaming at the top of his lungs, "Ice cream! Ice cream!"

What do you do? Do you stop and ponder the possibility that the ice cream man is indeed coming and that he does indeed have ice cream in his truck? Do you judge whether or not you can spare the calories? No! You'd be a sick little kid if you did! You drop your stick, turn around, and run straight at the ice cream man and indulge in creamy goodness.

Now, I am not suggesting that we have a child-ish faith. That is something completely different than childlike faith. Childish faith is believing in something that you have no good reason to believe. When we were kids, this would include the monster under the bed. As Christians, childish faith is exhibited when we believe but we do not know <u>why</u> we believe or even have a good grasp on <u>what</u> we believe, either.

Childlike faith is much different, therefore, from child-ish faith as one is devoid of suspicion, cynicism, and malice, while the other is devoid of any intellect. Therefore, guys, let's stay away from being childish. We Christians get so wrapped up in petty matters that we should at least avoid petty thinking. Paul said that, "When I was a child, I spoke as a child, I understood as a child, I thought as a child. But when I became a man, I put childish things aside." In the same manner, let's put aside our childish faith and strive for a more adult faith that is grounded in the Scriptures.

CHAPTER 4:

Hope

Hope does not seem like much. In our society, faith is scorned and hope is ignored. We say "I have faith in you" to encourage a person when they are ready to jump off the bridge, but when we say "I hope he won't kill himself," well, we don't expect much.

Therefore, our society sees some value in faith, but it does not put much stock in hope. Hope is a crutch and a weakness. It is delusional. This thinking is ridiculous. Very few things in this world are more amazing than hope. Sure, faith and love are cool. Faith brings us to God and shows us who He is. We cannot please God without faith, and love is awesome, because none of our actions on earth matter if we do not act out in love, but hope is the building block on which faith must be built and on which love grows.

Oddly, the three work together. Paul said (in 1 Corinthians, chapter 13) that there were three things that remain in our Christian walks that are of essential importance: faith, hope, and love, and that the greatest of these is love. I suggest that these three things are a progressive maturing from the first experience – faith – to the last, which is love.

First, a person has faith. He believes that Jesus died for his sins, rose again on the third day, and then declares Jesus to be the Lord (Master) over his (the sinner's) life. At this point, theological mysteries and what-not do not really matter. Simple faith has saved the man.

After a little while, the man grows and reads some of the Bible. He sees passages like "I go to prepare a place for you, and if I go and prepare a place for you, I will come again and receive you to Myself, that where I am, you may be also," and then he reads Paul's and John's writings about Heaven and he realizes that something better is coming. Our new believer's faith has grown. It has expanded and has become "hope." Through faith he believes that it is possible and through hope he wants it to happen. For reasonable hope to exist, faith has to exist.

Unreasonable hope comes in wishes: "Gee, I sure wish we could all just get along." Reasonable hope comes through a reasonable faith, based on facts and patterns that have already been established: "I hope that my son, whom I have trained well and whom I have been praying for, will become a Christian someday."

Now that our new believer has placed his faith in Christ and is looking forward to the glory of Heaven, he begins to look deeper into his new beliefs. He reads that God loves him. He reads that God is great and worthy to be praised. He reads that God died so that he could live with God forever because God wanted to be with him. Eventually, the man's faith (which led him to believe God existed) mingles with his hope (that he will one day meet God), and he begins to love the God that he has been reading about.

It's not impossible to assume this, even in a secular sense. I see the commercials advertising for Match.com and other matchmaking websites. They describe a way to meet someone that involves faith (the belief that the person you are talking to on the other end actually exists, and is actually interested in you and is not stringing you along), hope (that you will one day meet this "perfect person.") and then, eventually, love (you correspond and through correspondence, you come to love the person, or, at least, the person that you hope that they are).

Christianity is the same way, only without that smiling guy on the commercials that wants you to reach true compatibility.

Now, all this is to say that in Hebrews, Chapter 11, verse 1, faith is described as the substance of things hoped for and the evidence of things unseen. In other words, we see that hope precedes faith. In other words, the things we hope for are given substance by faith. In other words, it's as though hope is the soul of the body and faith is the flesh.

Faith is the certainty that what we want is more than a pipe dream; it separates the things that we want from the things we truly believe in. Faith gives body to hope and is, in that way, superior to it. In many instances, faith and hope are synonymous or, at least, are seen to be symbiotic to each other; one feeding off the other and both growing in proportion.

I include this little qualifier so that no one may point to certain verses in the Bible and claim that I did not acknowledge faith's relation to hope.

But I have just spent the first few pages of this chapter describing the trinity of the chief Christian virtues (faith, hope, love), and have not really delved into what this chapter is about and why it is so important to the Christian.

First, a bit of background. Two thousand years ago, Jesus said that Christians would not have an easy time in this world. If the world hated Jesus, it would hate us, too, because the world likes to shoot the messengers. Our message is simple: people are sinners and are going to Hell, but God does not want them to go to Hell, so He sent Jesus to save them from Hell, but also to make it possible for humans to know God as a man knows his friend. This good news appears to be foolish to those that are perishing; to those who have no desire to know about God. To everyone else, the Gospel rocks.

Anyway, as mentioned above, Jesus said life would be tough for the Christian, but He said that He would be with us, even until the ending of the age (Matthew 28:20). Paul went on to say that trials, tribulations, and troubles were a good thing because these tough times bring to mind that our citizenship is not on earth but is in Heaven. Our hopes should not be pinned upon these perishable things, but should be centered on the imperishable.

There is an old saying that there are some people walking around that are too heavenly-minded to be of any earthly-good. I think this is the stupidest phrase I have ever heard. I was sitting in a church when I was first introduced to this idea.

At the time, I was a little kid and didn't think much about it. After a few years of being taught mindless Christianity, my family and I changed churches and learned that there is no such thing as being "too" focused on Heaven in fact, having a heavenly mindset is not only helpful to the Christian, it is vital!

Let's face it, people. This world is terrible. We have terrorists threatening us left and right, we have the fear that our president will either not react or react too strongly, we fear that our children will grow up to follow the emo clique, or something worse (if you don't know what emo-ism is, parents, then you haven't been paying enough attention to what your kids are most likely watching), and we fear that we are going to fail at something and everyone will hate us: our lives are full of fear.

We Christians have several options available to us. We can get caught up in the fear and go completely paranoid. We can ignore the fear that we feel. We can accept that we're afraid and join a cult. Or we can do the biblical thing and put our hope in the fact that Heaven is coming, it is coming soon, and it is going to rock. I'm not talking robes, harps, and pink clouds. No, that's a stupid myth that Satan has perpetuated to make you think Heaven is going to be boring.

Think of everything good that you currently enjoy on this earth. Think of that without the taint of sin. Now think of enjoying all that in the presence of God.

In Heaven, I may actually be a good baseball player. In Heaven, I will probably get to see a grand tour of the stars and nebulae that are scattered throughout the galaxy. Eventually, when Heaven comes down to the New Earth (Check the last couple of chapters in Revelation), I'll get to reign with Jesus. How could what we call "Heaven" possibly be boring?

Hope is not "wishful thinking," but is the anticipation that, when someone has made a promise to us, they will fulfill their promise. Jesus made a promise to us. He told us that He was preparing a place for us and that He would be coming back to get us so that we could always be with Him. Our hope does not rest in what some preacher tells us; our hope does not reside in the musty tomes of the Church fathers; our hope does not thrive on the titillating thrill we get when we are in the presence of God. No, our faith rests in what Jesus Himself told us: that Heaven exists, that He's coming to take us there, and He will be with us there forever.

CHAPTER 5:

And the Greatest of These....

"Beloved, let us love one another, for love is of God; and everyone who loves is born of God and knows God. He who does not love does not know God, for God is love." (1 John 4:7-8)

There we go. Enough said. Book can end right there.

In an ideal world, that would be true. This world is far from ideal, however, and I need something to fill my evenings with, so I will expound a bit.

The English language is a simplistic tongue which does not allow for many different words that convey a variety of emotions and feelings. For example, the English word, "love." It's a terrible word. For example; I love ice cream. I prefer the kind made with a chocolate-caramel swirl. I always order Gold Medal Ribbon ™ from Baskin Robbins (C).

Likewise, I love my mom and dad.

I also love my friends.

I also love my dog (assuming I had one, which I do not).

I also will love my wife, when she finally shows up (she is apparently a very slow-moving individual).

I also love God.

You see? The English language does not provide me with enough of a lexicon to express the varying degrees wherein I love each of these groups of people/objects/Deity. Therefore, I have to delve into a little uneducated education in the Greek language, wherein the New Testament was written.

Many of us have read C.S. Lewis' book, *The Four Loves*. It is an excellent book that I would recommend to anyone that is trying to learn as much as they can about God. In this book, Lewis takes particular care to describe four types of love that humans experience: affection, friendship, eros (romantic love), and charity.

Now, of course, if most of us are going to be honest with ourselves, we'll say that C.S. Lewis is so brilliant that we do not understand half of what he says. The man uses examples from ancient literature that boggle the mind and has a vocabulary that is daunting, to say the least. His book gives a fantastic description of the various loves that we encounter. However, this chapter is not a book review or summary, but is about one particular type of love.

The Definition of Love

The love that I'm talking about is called *agape,* what Lewis would call the "divine love." It's a weird word, and is hard to say: Ah-gah-pay. There. Now you have a reasonable pronunciation guide, without all the weird squiggly lines that are in a dictionary (who, aside from English teachers, really know what those lines even mean?)

Agape is a Greek word rarely used in any other type of Greek literature, and is never used in the positive fashion that the Bible uses it. The reason? *Agape* refers to a self-sacrificial love that puts another person's needs above one's own. In other words, when the English Bible says that "God is love," it is really saying that "God is an unrelenting, self-sacrificing love who gave everything away for the chance for you to be saved and come to love Him, too." However, that was way too long a sentence to put in the NKJV version of your Bible, so the translators opted to use the simplified version.

Another key word to note in the phrase "God is love" is the word "is." And, as Bill Clinton once said, the importance of the word depends on what your definition of "is" is.

In this case, "is" means that God makes up the very essence of what love (*agape*) is. It does not say "God is loving" or "God loves," but rather it states that God is the very essence of *agape*. The reverse, "love is God" is not true in the least, for love is but an aspect of who our God is and is not itself the dominating force in the universe.

God's love for us

The very nature of this kind of love is that it manifests itself towards that which is unlovely, which, by this course of logic, means that you are unlovely. Do a double-take. Yes, I said that. I went there. You are unlovely. The Bible says that all of humanity's goodness is like filthy rags to God. Before you were saved, you were wallowing in your sin (don't get me wrong, I was too). There was nothing noble or worthy of love in us. It was not an accident that made John Newton choose the words "Amazing grace, how sweet the sound, that saved a <u>wretch</u> like me (emphasis mine)." Grace is amazing – *agape* love is amazing – because it is given to those that do not deserve it, merit it, or are worthy of it.

Grace is so amazing, as described by the apostle Paul who discusses how picky people are about who they will give their lives for. Sometimes a person will die for a man that has it all together. Rarely, but still possible, will a person die for a man that has some problems, maybe smokes some crack, but still a generally good guy. However, no one would ever die for a rapist, a terrorist, or a murderer. God did. He shows us what love is when He came to earth and died for the unlovely elements of society. When He died for sinners. When he died for you and for me. He showed us how to love, a capacity that was born into us, but lays dormant until a person is saved (Romans 5:7-8).

The Imago Dei

I personally believe that this is what was meant when it was said that God made Man in His own image. I hypothesize that this means that the very image in which Man was created was the capacity for *agape* love. Why do I think this? Because I do not believe we see angels exhibiting love; exhibiting the kind of freewill sacrifice that leads to a person dying for another – especially dying for someone who is an imperfect being; a rebel against God. Why don't I think that angels are capable of love? Because angels were not created to be companions or friends of God, but it was clearly stated that they were created to be His servants, created to live entirely to do His bidding (Psalm 104:4). In other words, they cannot love because their purpose for God does not demand that they be able to love.

Maybe I'm wrong about angels. I certainly could be since there is very little data for us to draw from. I am speculating, and nothing more. On the nature of angels and the exact definition of how we are made in God's image, (imago Dei), you'll have to either agree with me or research books of Christian theology, or compose your own theory, for I don't think the Bible is too clear on that issue.

What does this mean for us? Possibly one of the most painful messages in Christianity. *Agape* love loves that guy in the other cubicle; the one who refuses to wear deodorant. *Agape* love loves the Christian that acts like he is so much better than you because God blessed him with a Ferrari and a million of dollars, while all you have is a mobile home and a dog named Bleu. *Agape* love loves the people who are unlovely in our lives; who hurt us, either deliberately or carelessly.

All of these people will eventually get theirs, for God says that He will defend the orphan and the widow, the oppressed and downtrodden. Granted, you may not see results in this life, but it will happen. God will eventually handle all the corruption and wickedness that you see around you, but it is our job – yours and mine – to love these people, especially when they are undeserving of that love.

That word, "undeserving" is a tricky one. We think of other people as "undeserving," but we rarely turn our gaze inward and realize that we are undeserving of God's love, too. We don't merit the fancy mansion that Jesus says he's building for us. We have not earned the right to call God, "Papa." We cannot pay back the debt that allows us to be pulled out of Hell.

You think Osama bin Laden is unlovely? Adolph Hitler? Genghis Kahn? Well, you are just as unlovely. Sure, you may not have blown up buildings, or started a war that caused tens of millions to die, or ravaged Europe with your Mongol horde, but you have blown up at your kids, started petty fights that degenerated into hating another person, ravaged a person's soul by saying uncouth things about them. You and I are horrible people that are just as guilty of sinning against God as humanity's greatest offenders.

If we want to look at all the undeserving people that God loves, then we can look at the Bible in Hebrews 11 to see a list of some of the most degenerate people in all history. Jacob lied and cheated his brother out of his rightful inheritance; Moses was a murderer; Rahab was a hooker; Gideon created an idol; Barak was a coward; Samson was a man who had everything given to him, but he violated all of his vows; Jephthah sacrificed his daughter; David killed people when he couldn't get his way; Jeremiah whined; Jonah fled his responsibilities and pouted when God chose to be merciful rather than destroy an entire city...the list goes on. These flawed, broken people are loved by God and, through their faith in God and in His promises, they went on to do great things. God loves people that are flawed, people that are broken, because if He didn't love the broken people, there would be no one to love.

Maybe you'll never do anything "terrible" in your life. Perhaps you'll be one of those lucky men that remain faithful to his wife for all 43.4 years of marriage. Perhaps you'll not beat your kid. Perhaps you won't kill your coworker for constantly being cheerful on Monday mornings. Congrats for that. You'll save yourself a world of hurt, but you're still unlovely. If you look at yourself in comparison to the righteousness of Jesus, then you'll see that you really aren't the paragon of virtue that you wish you were.

The Responsibility of Love

Sometimes love is hard and inconvenient for us. It may involve going to our best friend and say, "Look, [insert name here], I want you to know that I love you, but you are coming across as a very arrogant individual, and I don't want that to hurt your testimony to other people." Love involves rebuke. How do we know this? The Bible says that those whom He loves, He chastens. It goes on further to explain why; because we are His adopted sons. A father only disciplines his legitimate children, the ones He loves and expects something from. The only children that are not disciplined are bastards (in the literal sense, not the pejorative sense). Bastards are either pampered and coddled or beaten and ignored because they will never have the responsibilities that a trueborn heir will have.

Now, obviously, we are not God, so we do not have the right to go to [insert name here] and say "Look, you've been acting like a jerk lately, so I am going to have to sneeze on you until you get the cold I have been having so that you may be properly reprimanded for your actions." That's just wrong and a bit gross. However, we can warn people and correct them in love, because, honestly, we don't want their sinning to come to the point where God has to punish them to get them to come back to Him. It may come to that, but that is for God to decide (Disclaimer: Before you correct a person, pray hard. You may find that God has another way of dealing with a person and does not want to get you involved. And some Christians get really, REALLY annoyed when a person tries to correct them and will rebel against any well-intentioned advice. Sometimes praying for a person is the best thing you can do.).

Likewise, love involves telling nonbelievers about Jesus. "For God so loved the world that…" you know the rest. God loved the world, became a man, and died the death of an innocent man so that we might come to Him. "For this is love, that while we were still sinners, Christ died for us." Therefore, if God loved us enough to die for us, when He had every right to hate us, then we ought to love others enough to tell them about what He did.

This is the easiest and hardest part of Christianity. Witnessing. It sends shudders down some people's spines as they fear that they can never tell another person something so controversial…however, we feel fine telling a person why we think so-and-so would make a much better candidate than what's-his-face. The former conversation is of eternal significance, while the latter conversation is of no significance (seriously. Christianity > Politics).

I believe that there is good reason to suspect that the reason we fear to witness to our friends/families/whoever God tells us to is because the Enemy does not want us to witness. I suggest this is for several reasons. First, and most importantly, when a person hears about the Gospel of Christ, that person is presented with the opportunity to receive the gift of salvation that Christ offers all mankind. The Enemy does not want people to be saved. It's not because he can have eternity to torment these souls in Hell, but I believe he does it out of his spite and hatred for God. Every soul that goes to Hell is a soul that chose to rebel against God to the very end, just like Satan did.

Imagine that the Devil is this little kid and God is this really, really tall man with long arms and huge hands. The little kid tries to run up and punch the tall man, but can't even reach his knee. All the tall man has to do is put his arm on the kid's head, and the little tike can't even reach him. That's kinda the way it is between God and Satan…amplified about a billion times. If the little kid wanted to hurt the man, he must find what he values most and destroy it, since he cannot directly damage this large man.

So, if the Devil cannot hurt God, he does the next best thing and takes down the ones God loves the most…us.

Therefore, this "War between good and evil" that people are always talking about is not a conventional war in that there is the possibility that evil might overcome good. Rather, this is a war of attrition. How many casualties can the devil inflict before God puts an end to it all?

Why does God allow this battle for our souls to wage on? Why does He allow billions of men and women to decide to go to Hell, thus giving the Devil another minor victory? Because love demands choices.

Love's Great Choice

Let's put it this way. Let us assume that I was in this area of the world where every man for miles has a face like Quasimodo. In this area, however, is this one beautiful woman. If that woman were to see me among all these hideous faces - even though mine isn't much to look at - she'd have no real choice. If, however, she were in the middle of Spain, where (so I hear) the men are more attractive than in any other nation in Europe, then she would have hundreds upon thousands of choices that she could make. If said female were to take an interest in me while we were in the land of the ugly people, then it means nothing, since there is no one else to compare me to, and she would likely dump me as soon as she sees a more attractive face. If, however, she were to pick me over all of Spain, then I would feel truly loved and special.

The analogy - though imperfect and a bit silly - illustrates that, for love to be genuine, it has to be given an alternative. God knew this, and in creating Man, gave him the freedom to choose between God and Man's own self. Yeah. We're so narcissistic that we would love ourselves over God. Go figure.

Satan's role is to encourage us to love ourselves over God. Let's look at the Garden of Eden. We know the story. God made man and woman, put them in this beautiful garden with two rules: subdue the earth by making babies and don't eat from the Tree of the Knowledge of Good and Evil. We have no idea how long it took them to "get it on," but we imagine that Adam was a little bit shy at first. What we do know, however, is that Eve was chilling around the tree, maybe trying to get a better look at the fruit she wasn't supposed to eat, possibly wondering why God didn't want them to eat from the tree when the fruit looked <u>so</u> appetizing.

Enter Satan.

Satan, disguised as a serpent, comes to the woman and says, as if he were reading her mind, "Has God <u>really</u> said that you can't eat of every tree in the garden?" Satan begins by misquoting God, as is his modus operandi. Eve follows suit by misquoting God by saying that he had told Adam and Eve that they could not even touch the fruit, or they would die. (side note: This, people, is why it is important to know exactly what God says. Eve did not; she misquoted Him, she was led astray, and humanity got the shaft.)

Satan seizes the opportunity and says that she would surely not die and goes on to imply that God was lying to her because the fruit of the Tree would make them like God, and God wanted to keep all His power to Himself. Eve liked the idea of being like God. She liked the idea of being <u>equal</u> with God. Of being a god herself. Therefore, she ate the fruit, gave some to Adam (who was standing right next to her, doing nothing), and God cast them out of the

Garden, condemned them to eventual death, made childbearing insanely painful for all women and made men to work the grounds and sweat out the ability to provide for their families. Satan got the worst punishment, for God then prophesied that Eve's seed (Jesus) would crush Satan's head.

As you see, the very first man and woman chose themselves over God. But that is the consequence of love. God knew it when He created us. He knew that the major majority of humanity would not choose Him and that humans would do terrible things to other people in an effort to slake their lust for power.

This is an area where I cannot understand the mind of God. He deemed it worthy – nay, necessary – for mankind to be fitted with both the capacity for *agape* love and the free will that would allow mankind to ignore and suppress that God-given gift.

And this is where love takes a tough spin for us. God knew many wouldn't choose Him – let's make a nice, even estimation of 80% of humanity throughout history have not chosen Him – but He deemed it worth the loss. 20% of mankind was enough for Jesus to come down to earth, shed immortality to don mortality, die an innocent death, and rise from the dead three days later.

Why doesn't God just redeem those other 80%? He is love, isn't He? What kind of loving God would force people to go to Hell instead of just redeeming them? If you think this, then you are only reading part of the story and are getting only part of God's character description. God is not only love, but He is holy, just, and true. Sin cannot stand in His presence, therefore it must reside elsewhere. God's holiness demands that this be so. Sin cannot remain unpunished, so it must be dealt with. God's justice demands that this be so. Sin cannot be covered up and lied about to make everyone feel better. God's veracity demands that this be so. Therefore, since sin cannot be covered up, lied about, or go unpunished, God must judge each and every human being by their own righteousness.

The problem is our righteousness is flawed. It is as dirty rags, remember? It is disgusting in God's sight because He knows all of our ulterior motives in doing good deeds and, what's worse, He knows the sin that taints these acts, making them damaged goods. He sees our rebellion and our overt choosing of ourselves over Him. The only way that God's justice, holiness, and veracity can be appeased is by interposing God's love. Only Jesus can save us from our sin, but it is a personal choice that must be made. No 12-step book can save you; you cannot discover your "life's purpose" and count on that to save you; you cannot become a better you and discover a brand new tomorrow. No, you have to, you HAVE to receive the gift of cleansing from your sins before you can step into Heaven and request that Jesus be made Master over your life before salvation can be yours.

God's love is so powerful that it can overcome God's justice, holiness, and veracity, but human will can overcome God's love in that a person can refuse to accept God's love. All over the Bible, the authors are pleading with people to come to Christ, to choose to be forgiven and forsake their sins. But God will not spiritually force Himself on a person. He is no rapist, but is a gentleman. If you do not choose to receive the gift He offered you, then you have chosen Hell, and there are no two ways around it.

I understand that this chapter goes against the Calvinist doctrine of God's absolute sovereignty over salvation, but I cannot deny what my own experience of God and understanding of the Bible seems to say: man has a choice, even though God knows who will choose Him and who will reject Him.

Sins forgiven + Jesus as Lord of your life = Relationship with God and avoidance of Hell. You don't get saved because you want your life to be better or as a way to overcome addiction. You become a Christian because you have been made aware of the need for Jesus. Anything less than a total acknowledgement of personal sin and exalting Jesus to His rightful place in your life is a Christianity that is flawed.

If you are a believer, then, if there is anything you should take from this chapter, it is this: The first and greatest commandment: Love the Lord your God with all your heart, with all your soul, and with all your mind. The second: Love your neighbor as yourself. Easy as cake (I know the phrase is "easy as pie," but it is not easy to make pie. The analogy is flawed.).

In the previous chapter, we discussed Paul's statement in 1 Corinthians 13, "And now abide faith, hope, and love, these three; but the greatest of these is love."

For someday, our faith and hope will be irrelevant, for we shall one day see Him in whom we have placed our faith and our hope shall be realized. We shall have no more need for faith and hope when all the prophesies have been fulfilled and we stand in the presence of Jesus. However, for all eternity, love will remain as we love God and each other.

Truly the poets were right when they said that love is eternal..

CHAPTER 6:

A Humbling Experience

I often hear from Christians, "Never ask God for humility unless you know what you're asking, because when He humbles you, you get hammered." This idea troubles me. To most of us, this statement implies that God is sitting up in Heaven thinking, "I cannot wait [God doesn't use contractions] for one of those snot-nosed humans to beg me for humility. I am going to nail them to the <u>wall</u>!!!" We inadvertently paint God as a monster and are sending a horribly tainted view of prayer: "Be careful what you wish for."

The view that God will stick it to a person if they ask for humility implies at least three major errors. First, this view portrays God as a sadist who loves to torment humans. Second, this view implies that you should be fearful of praying to God because you never know what He is going to do to you if you ask the wrong thing. Finally, this view seems to imply that prayer is a type of wish-fulfillment.

Well, let me be perfectly clear: God is not a monster, you shouldn't fear praying to God for anything, and prayer is <u>not</u> wish-fulfillment.

In the Bible, we read verses that emphasize the importance of humility, specifically before God; (paraphrased) "You are God in Heaven, here am I on earth, so let my words be few,(Eccl 5:2)" "I had heard of You, but now that I see You, I abhor myself (Job 42:5,6)," "Humble yourself in the sight of the Lord and He will lift you up

(James 4:10)," and so on. The Bible makes it very clear to us that humility before God is important, and Solomon, David, and the rest of the authors in the Bible make it clear to us that God "lifts up the humble [and] He casts the wicked down to the ground (Psalm 147:6)."

All we have to do is look at history to see examples of the proud being humbled and the humble being exalted. We can look at all the dictators in history to see men that were very proud. In most cases, dictators were men that created or united a country out of a bunch of warring, or, at least, unpleasant states. These men were proud in their accomplishments, but rather than give glory to God, they gave glory to themselves.

Stalin created a cult of personality, the Caesars made themselves to be gods, and Nebuchadnezzar looked at the glory of the great Babylonian Empire and refused to bow the knee before God. However, Stalin died a painful death, either by suicide or at the hands of an assassin. The Caesars nearly all died ignominious deaths, either by suicide, by assassins, or by usurpers. And Nebuchadnezzar, creator of one of the greatest empires on earth, was driven insane until he would lift up his eyes to Heaven and declare that Yahweh was God.

At the same time, David did not seek to be king, but was one of the most successful monarchs in history, as he had conquered all the kingdoms that tried to fight him, and even had mighty nations like Egypt paying him tribute so that he would not invade. David humbled himself like few other men, and God honored him. Even when David allowed pride to creep in, and God punished him, David's heart remained on God and was known as a man after God's own heart.

So, we know that God is great and if we are honest with ourselves, we know that we are not. This is a pretty humble attitude. Why, then, the need for more humility? Why don't we Christians just act humble because we know that God is much better than us and that He always has been and He always will be? It should be second nature for us, shouldn't it? It can't be, because our sinful nature still exists and it always whispers to us that we know better than God.

Think about it. You and I go through our day making dozens of decisions every 24 hours. Some of these decisions are important and some are trivial. How often do we ask for God's will when it comes to the important decisions and how often do we simply choose the path that seems right to us instead?

Paul said in Romans that we are dead to sin, alive to Christ, and this makes it so that we can enter into a relationship with Christ. HOWEVER, in the same book, Paul says that we will all keep on sinning, even after Jesus has come into our lives. Paul called it a great confusion that he did not do what he wanted to do – which was live for God – but he sinned, which he did not want to do. He goes on to call himself the chief among sinners. If I were a psychologist (thank God that I am not), I would say that Paul had negative self-image issues and probably was not hugged enough as a child. Since I am not a psychologist, I shall instead say that Paul had a good view of his own sinfulness which led him to a better understanding of himself with relation to God and other people.

Obviously, with our continual imperfection, we Christians will never stop sinning until we reach Heaven. If Paul was bemoaning his sinful state, even until the time of his death, then what hope do we have of ever thinking that we are better than the man that penned half of the New Testament? For the Christian, there is no place for pride. First of all, comparing ourselves to another Christian is a misleading standard; it doesn't matter if I am a better person than Ted Bundy, because I am still a worm when compared to God.

Therefore, I ought to be humble, both in the sight of God and in the sight of man. My human nature – the part of me that remains inherently sinful– will keep wanting to sin, even when my spirit – which has been brought to life by Jesus – is crying out for me to avoid sin like the plague that it is.

So that's why we have to pursue humility; because we remain sinners, even with the restorative work of Christ.

But what's so bad about asking God to be humble? Well, a lot of Christians cynically say that it is the one prayer that God is sure to answer. This is not true. As I read my Bible, there are two things that God will give to all without prejudice: wisdom and His Spirit.

The Bible does not say that He will unfailingly answer every request to be made humble or that He will recklessly give us whatever we want. God will do what He wants in His own time.

It is good for a man to ask for humility. It shows humility itself for him to be willing to ask to be made humble before God and meek before men. By pursuing humility, the man of God is pursuing the mindset of Christ, who humbled Himself and became obedient to the point of death, even death on a cross.

Just because we pray for humility, we should never assume that God is a genie that will jump at our command, or that He is longing for a request to be made so that He can fulfill it in the most painful way possible. God will answer our requests, and it will sometimes be in a manner that we could not expect, and the answer can be painful, but God does not take glee in human suffering as we seem to imply that He does.

God is not sitting up in Heaven hoping we'll pray for "the wrong thing" and then give it to us because He is obligated to grant our prayer requests (like a genie). In fact, Jesus addresses this claim by saying, "If you, who are wicked, give good things to your children, how much more will God give to those that ask Him?"

Let me restate that for those of you that have been skimming: if we give good things to our kids, then God, who is so much better than us, will give better gifts when it is asked of Him.

Of course, we don't always know what is best or when the timing is right. Let's look at it this way. In showing that God gives good gifts, He draws a comparison to the behavior of earthly fathers. If a son asks a father for a loaf of bread, the father will not give him a snake. What if, however, the boy asks for a snake? Will the father, knowing that the snake is bad for the boy, give it to him anyway? Of course not! That father would be a horrible individual and should be shot! In the same way, we don't always know what is best for us, but God does.

Therefore, our prayer life (which will be covered in greater detail in a later chapter) should reflect this understanding:

"God, I know you already know what I want before I ask, but this is what I need. Please provide, if it be in Your will, and let me accept whatever Your will may be, for You know best." This is but a poor example; if you want true examples of humility, examine Daniel's prayer for forgiveness for Israel, or David's humility through the Psalms, or in Jesus' example in the famous "Lord's Prayer." With these examples in hand, we may know what it is to be humble before our God.

CHAPTER 7:

A Theory on Relativity

It is unfortunate that there are very few honest moral relativists. These are the people that say, "There are no moral absolutes in any circumstance." Most "moral relativists" cheat a bit by saying "Morals are defined by society." This is a much less honest and much less interesting belief.

It is less honest because the early moral relativists would actually say what they meant, even if it were widely unpopular, and would risk going against the facts, just because they believed something to be true. This theory was easily disproved when someone were to, say, steal the relativist's stereo. The moral relativist cannot claim that the thief did something wrong because the thief was acting in accordance with his own moral code. The belief that morals come from society is less interesting because a person had to have been a bit insane to believe that there are no moral absolutes of any kind.

Look around you and imagine if we lived in a world where everyone felt it was ok to kill anyone else and they were never punished for it. I'm not talking about a sadistic government regime that tortures its civilians; I am talking about nationwide anarchy of a catastrophic proportion. .

Now, the societal relativists, with their less interesting and less honest beliefs, are still trying for the same goal as the other fellows: to try to give justification for their disbelief in a just God who has set forth moral absolutes that He demands be obeyed. Morality almost always revolves around sex.

"Who are you to say that homosexuality is wrong? That's just your morality."

"What do you mean I can't sleep with my boyfriend? My professor says it's a healthy expression of our sexuality!"

If you've ever been a Christian in college, you've probably heard these statements and groaned a little bit because you probably knew that this person was just providing an excuse for getting it on with whomever he so chooses.

So what's the big deal with a society-driven morality? It sounds attractive, from a humanistic perspective. As Mankind evolved, it eventually came up with a set of guidelines that ensured that it was possible for Man to live in harmony with each other. Anytime society changes, morality changes. Old moralities are discarded for the new moralities.

So...what about the reformers of an old moral system? What about the ones that did what society thought was morally wrong and unpopular and violated the societal norms? What about William Wilberforce, who fought slavery in England? What about Martin Luther King, Jr., who showed us that race didn't make a man different from another man, or his namesake, Martin Luther, who stated that a church should not try to fleece the people that place themselves under its authority? These men are regarded as heroes because they showed us Truth. Each appealed to something deep within men to make them realize that something was wrong with the way things currently were and that the reformer's way was right.

These are three men who were revolutionaries against the commonly held beliefs of society and each should have been destroyed before their views took hold and spread through society.

Instead, their views touched society at large and showed that the common practice - the socially acceptable norm - was wrong. They appealed to a greater sense of morality, to a moral Absolute, and that Absolute was God and that His morality was relayed to us through the Spirit and through the Bible. For transgressing the norms of society, they should have their names stricken from the history books. If moral relativism were true, then the reforms that these men sought should be ignored by the more highly evolved, for society deemed that slavery was acceptable, that discrimination was laudable, and that simony and indulgences were commendable.

There is no benefit to society or to Darwinian survival of the fittest theory if one claims that all men are created equal. If a group of people were too weak to survive the onslaught of a stronger nation, then they should be made to service the strong, according to this strict social Darwinism. However, no one claims these things because they know that it is not true. Those that do adhere to these beliefs eventually support men like Adolf Hitler and ideas such as eugenics, and become capable of the worst atrocities that mankind has seen.

But I digress...

However, I have to be honest with you; this is not a chapter about defending moral relativity from pagans. There is literature by the truckload on how to debunk a relativist and they in turn have literature on how to debunk Christianity. It's a wonderful circle of pain and frustration that will end in a second Inquisition, this time directed against all Christians and Jews and Muslims (the three religions that dictate absolutes) rather than against Protestants or Jews. I digress.

This chapter's main purpose is to look you, the Christian, in the eye and explain that God's morality does not change for us just because we are saved.

I have had some non-believing friends ask me what the Christian's stance was on a Christian having premarital sex since the Christian has been saved by grace, and is no longer going to Hell.

Paul, in the letter to the Romans, asked if, since we are saved by grace, should we be allowed to sin more so that God may be more glorified by saving us from more sin? Paul's response to this rhetorical question: "Certainly not!" Grace came to us so that we could live in freedom from sin, not fall back into it.

To say that we are free to ignore the morality of the Bible - which includes the popular restrictions, like don't murder, as well as the unpopular ones, like don't use any crude language or jokes - just because we are saved is like saying that you should jump off the Empire State Building, just because you have a hang glider. Sound like a good idea? Not really. You'll get torn to shreds by the wind or you'll slam into a building. It's the same way with trying to fly by the radar of your own morality rather than with the moral compass of the Bible.

For instance, when it comes to relative morality, Christians take 9/10 of the commandments very seriously. We love God above all else, we keep the Sabbath (well, most of the time), we don't commit adultery (except for the occasional mental fantasy), we have yet to kill someone (although that *@#$&! that cut me off on the freeway sure deserves a good beating), but we forget…to…not…covet. Lo and behold, a chink in the Christian armor!

The Digression Continues

What does it mean to covet (and how has this chapter gone from moral relativity to covetousness)? To covet something is to want something that you have no business wanting, either because someone else has it or simply because you don't have it. For instance…well, look at our society. Thanks to the zeal of the advertising industry, we average people are told that we are incomplete because we do not have the right gadget, or that our lives are meaningless because our doodads are out of date, or we are shameful human beings because our bodies are not sculpted like those of the Greek gods. Video games, cars, new "Just for her" deodorant, and food, food, food.

We are told that we want these things – that we <u>need</u> these things – when, in reality, we should be content in all circumstances, whether in plenty or in poverty, just like Paul was. We should not say that, "Well, I've held off on lust today, so I'm going to indulge in a bit of gluttony. I'm going to eat a $5 pizza from Little Caesar's." I say this from personal experience; I did this at my fraternity.

Gluttony and covetousness have to be the top two sins we Christians tend to ignore, and they are, of course, detrimental to us. First of all, gluttony is the desire to have more than you need. It does not necessarily extend to food, but we see it more readily in the fact that a good portion of America's churchgoers are above the healthy weight for their height. Or, if you prefer the blunt terminology: We. Are. Fat.

However, gluttony also extends to an overzealous obsession to purchase shoes (women, you do not need 30 pairs of shoes. That's gluttonous and insane.) Men, you do not need to own that new 1911 Colt pistol if you already have five others.

Covetousness is when we look at Bill Gates and we see his money and we say, "Hey. That money should be mine." Uh oh...looks like I strayed into the realm of a political hornet's nest...well, let's be honest with ourselves, brothers and sisters; when we see someone doing well, we are inclined to think one of three things: "He's doing well, I feel glad for him (minority view)," "He's doing well, I want to achieve as much as him and have the power that he has (slightly less minority view)," or "Where's Robin Hood to take away from the rich and give to the poor...meaning me (the view of the majority)?"

People, we need to stop looking outward and wanting more (I drive a Toyota Camry. So what?); stop looking inward and finding our perceived inadequacies and start looking upward again. Nowhere in the Bible does it say that all will be equitable on earth. Even when Jesus returns, there will be different rewards and gifts for different people and no one even knows what that will be like.

To Tie it All Together

How does any of this tie into moral relativity? When we ignore sins like gluttony and covetousness, we are saying that sins like adultery are wrong, but that sins like glutting and coveting are ok because...well, I guess it's because we've stopped thinking of them as wrong. We are bred from the womb to think that it is natural to want more and, in more recent times, we are taught to hate the rich for being wealthy. How dare they keep their money and not give all of it to the government which will, in turn, be more than fair in giving it to lower-class wage earners?

We cannot, we should not, we ought not look at one sin, declare it bad, and then forget the myriad other things in our lives that are damaging us. Take a look at your life, remove the plank from your own eye, and <u>then</u> begin to criticize everyone else for the speck of dust in their own eye, for then we find that our sins are relative in comparison to everyone else's.

CHAPTER 8

The Dangers of Zeal

"They zealously court you, but for no good; yes, they want to exclude you, that you may be zealous for them." (Galatians 4:17)

"But it is good to be zealous in a good thing always..." (Galatians 4:18)

Our society is leery around the word "zeal." It is a dangerous word because it often carries bad connotations. Zealous people blow up buildings, be they abortion clinics, World Trade Centers, Pentagons, churches, Spanish subways, Russian theaters and schools, etc, etc, etc. Zeal for one's religion (disguised as devotion) or for one's country (disguised as patriotism) can be very, very dangerous if the zeal is totally emotionally based and has overridden the rational parts of the brain. If a man feels that his passion exists above all else, including love for God and neighbor, than that man is a dangerous zealot, making his passion his idol.

Zeal is a type of emotional fervor that consumes a person. It can be described as love for the goal or religion that one is ascribing to. This kind of zeal can be a good thing, because zeal for country can lead a man to be proud of that for which his country stands and to defend it with fervor. A defense attorney is supposed to provide a "zealous defense" for his client, even if the accused is a criminal, which means that the attorney must do all he can to ensure that a man has a fair chance. A soldier that is zealous about warfare may be deadly effective on the battlefield and may follow orders with little to no questions, because he trusts in the wisdom of his superiors. A mother who is zealous in her love for her child will protect it at risk to her own life. A man who is zealous for God may step outside of where he is comfortable and talk about Jesus to a neighbor or friend. However, zeal can be misplaced and tragically so. Allow me to explain.

The 13th chapter of Paul's first letter to the Corinthians, Paul describes the dangers of the zealous Christian lifestyle by saying, "Though I speak with the tongues of men and of angels...though I have the gift of prophecy, and understand all mysteries and all knowledge, and though I have all faith, so that I could remove mountains but have not love, I am nothing."

What does this mean? Many very good and honest people do great works for God, such that they can "speak in tongues," or prophecy; some have faith to heal and to do great signs and wonders, but as soon as a Christian loses sight of love, then that Christian does not matter any longer and might as well stop talking about God, because he has lost his first love.

Many of the negatively zealous Christians that I know are young Christians, either they recently were saved or they recently became interested in the Gospel. If these men and women are poorly trained, then they can become dangerous and can harm the individual, people's perception of that individual, and people's perception of Christianity.

It all begins with the belief that you are right and everyone else is wrong. A Christian knows that his faith in Jesus is the only way to God, but if a Christian has not been brought up in love, then he can start to think poorly of nonbelievers and even snap at fellow Christians that follow a different set of beliefs.

The zealot does not usually act out of love towards his fellow man. He may love something, but it is not the *agape* love that Paul is talking about. More likely than not, the zealot loves himself but disguises that self-love as a form of love for God and will vehemently deny that he is doing anything but the will of God. The zealot is a showman who revels in the applause and attention of others. When he confronts a person of a differing faith, he is not afraid to show that his religion is right, but he is more anxious to score "points" than he is in showing love to the person and winning them to Christ.

The loveless zealot is more concerned about being right – be it about the proper usage of tongues, slaying in the spirit (good or bad), the proper translation of the Bible (what is it, really?), or the brand of toothpaste that best protects the mouth from plaque and gingivitis – and he will not take into account another person's feelings as long as he is right.

Paul was this kind of zealot. He was so zealous for the Law of Moses that he captured and executed Christians. It has been speculated (speculation, mind you; not guaranteed fact) that the rich, young ruler that Jesus had told to sell all of his goods may have been Paul (known as "Saul" at the time). If this is the case, then it is possible that he walked away from Jesus, disappointed, and then later jealous at His disciples and began to kill them. We see in some of his letters that Paul still feels guilt about the days before he was a Christian, but we also see him saying things like, "There is, therefore, now no condemnation for those who are in Christ Jesus." Paul turned his zeal around and instead of persecuting the Church, he began to zealously represent Christ as an ambassador; an approved workman, without need for shame because of his past.

I can empathize with the plight of the zealot because I have to fight the tendencies to be loveless in my zeal for the Lord. You see, I love being doctrinally right. I used to study apologetic after apologetic so that I would have the proper answer to any Muslim, Mormon or Jehovah's Witness. I didn't really care so much that they'd be saved as much as that I would prove to them that they were stupid and wrong. This attitude was reprehensible in the sight of God, because I understood mysteries, had faith to move mountains…but I did not have love, so I was nothing.

Therefore, I now tend to avoid religious debates as often as possible because I know my tendency to hurt others. I, as a weak man, thrive too much on the sport of debate and on the competition of winning, so, only when God prompts me, will I even consider challenging someone's beliefs.

Thus, out of my weakness I can speak with some authority: avoid the tendency to become a loveless zealot, because you will hurt those around you, you will hurt your reputation, and you will eventually hurt yourself.

Love God, first and foremost, and a love of people will follow. As Augustine said, "In the essentials, we must have unity, in the nonessentials, we must have liberty, but in all things, we must have charity."

As mentioned earlier, zeal, in and of itself, is not a bad thing. In fact, it is a very good thing. "It is good to be zealous in a good thing always." This is a powerful verse. It gives you and me permission to be (I shudder to use this Christian catch phrase) on fire for the Lord. Paul is essentially saying: "Look guys. You're going to Heaven. You know this was totally God's doing and not your own. So why are you moping about, saying that life is terrible? The people around you are dying and going to Hell and you know the only way that they can be saved. You should be so zealous that you should be crawling over burning-hot glass to talk to them."

And this is often a criticism against Christianity. If we believe that Jesus is who He says He is and that eternity will work out the way the Bible says it will (the righteous go to everlasting life, the unrighteous to everlasting damnation), then why are we not fulfilling the parable of the sower and the seeds and spreading the word out to whomever we can?

The parable shows a man spreading seeds all over this field. Unlike modern agriculture, the ancient method seemed to be more haphazard, though, admittedly, a lot more fun. You took a handful of seeds and chucked them into the wind. Some seeds fall on the paths that have been hardened and abused by other people's feet and are eaten by birds. Some fall among thorny bushes, where the growing plants choke and die. Some seeds fall in weak soil and die after a period of rapid growth. But some seeds fall in good soil and grow at an exponential rate.

Jesus spoke to crowds with this same parable. He was explaining the way that various people react to the Word of God, but I believe that this is also an example of how the Christian should witness: by spreading the Word of God wherever he can. This is true zeal. The zeal that says, "You know what? I'll bet nine out of ten seeds will not produce any fruit, but that one seed will take root, blossom and will spread like wildfire."

Now, I could be wrong about this method of witnessing and zeal. There do seem to be some among us that are better suited towards witnessing than others. Personally, I hate witnessing. I cannot hold two thoughts in my head at the same time and have an enormously difficult time getting past telling a person that Jesus loves them. Other people are so gifted that they set their fear aside and witness to cashiers at the fast food joints they go to, or they talk to homeless people and give them a job, a place to stay, and tell them about Jesus.

We cannot be deceived into thinking that witnessing to people should only come in this wildly noticeable manner. The Holy Spirit has commissioned some people to talk to crowds of nonbelievers and the Holy Spirit has commissioned some people to simply help an elderly shut-in who has no one that visits them and no one that seems to care anymore. Others will lead a life of peaceful witness to those around them, letting the way they conduct their lives be the example the World needs of what a good Christian should be like. These same people are quiet with their zeal. They love God, but they know that they are not evangelists. They still show His love, but they do it on the sly. Not talking to masses of people, but showing the practical, *agape* love side of Christianity. These are the quiet zealots who do the work of God, like the others, but act in more practical ministry than in evangelism.

To each according to his talents and his individual calling, for the Church is a Body that is made up of many parts, and if some can witness without words in their hometown, then we should encourage them and be glad that we have some that witness here at home.

Proper zeal takes many forms, but the root of all zeal should be love: love for God which will lead to a love for others.

Ken Dickason

CHAPTER 9

Depression

You know what? We all get depressed. Every one of us, man or woman, young or old, rich or poor, we look around at our lives and want something more. We are often discontent, sometimes for weeks at a time, finding ourselves inconsolable. The pagan may find himself turning to the vices that Christians ought not pursue. He may lose his mind in drugs, or find himself wrapped up in sex; he might seek a new, better paying job, or accumulate more power to slake his desire for that ever-present need for satisfaction. We Christians know these are not fulfilling and we know why.

We know that God is the ultimate fulfillment, but that may make our depression much more...severe. For us Christians, we have hope and we know about it. Therefore, when we get depressed, it is a very, very deep pain. Almost visceral, we feel the longing for home.

I fancy (though cannot prove) that the unbeliever feels the same dissatisfaction for the world that the Christian has, but he does not know why he cries. He may feel the tug for Home, but he does not know where Home is, what it is, or even how to reach it. We Christians know that we have been made for another place and we know that we want to be there. We know that we were originally designed to be perfect, but sin has corrupted that model. We know these things, but we also know that Jesus is soon coming back to right what is wrong and to redeem the earth. However, it seems so far away that our longing for Heaven remains, but we forget that Heaven is, in fact, what we are longing for.

Of course, herein lies the problem. We Christians, often without realizing it, wish so badly for Jesus to right the world that we find ourselves sinking into depression because of a lack in our surroundings, in our situation, in our life, and in the world itself, because we know that better was intended and better is coming. We are sad because we wish it were happening now. We find ourselves morose because Heaven is not yet on earth and will not be – according to the 21st chapter of Revelation – until the New Jerusalem descends from Heaven to find its final resting place on Earth.

We see around us horrible things. We see the Twin Towers falling, we hear of the riots that spring up, we see war everywhere we turn, and we see our heroes fail and fall all around us. Closer to home, we see our kids slowly turning away from the values we have taught them, we witness our friends abandoning their old faith, and we see, in ourselves, every sin and error we make. Even we Christians are not strong enough to hold back these tide waters!

And this is as it should be.

Depression is a great good for the Christian, or, rather, has the potential for being very good. Why on earth would I say such a thing? Because I myself was depressed when I first wrote this chapter. I was sad because I saw friends' faiths falter, I looked at the future and found it grim, and I looked to Jesus, and could not see Him because my own sin was clouding my vision. I was depressed because I could not hear His voice, but it was not for any lack of love on His part, but because my ears had become clogged with my own self righteousness. It was only when I became depressed at my circumstances that I saw the failings in myself.

The Bible says that Jesus forgives all sins past, present, and future, but our sins can keep us from hearing what He is saying to us. It can keep us from knowing His will.

We have always heard that communication is a two-way road, and it's true. God is constantly talking to us; the Word of God has never stopped speaking, but we often stop up our own ears from listening. I do it. At the time I wrote this, I did not want to hear God's will about something. I wanted to do things my way and I was holding tightly to what I thought were my rights and my needs. God was merciful, however, and sent me a deep depression, so that I might examine what was wrong…and find that I had an infection. That infection was the disease of self. I was wanting my own will so badly that I refused to allow God His proper throne in my life.

And that is depression's purpose. I believe that depression is God's way of saying one of two things: "Ken, there is something wrong here that I want to fix," or "Ken, I want you to remember that this world is not your home; I want you to remember that I am waiting for you."

Some will say "God would never want you to be sad; depression is an attack by the devil." Yeah, the devil probably is behind some of it. Of course, we know from the story of Job and of Joseph that what the enemy means for our detriment, God means for our betterment. The devil is a roaring lion, seeking whom he might devour, and God will string him along to allow him to tempt and test us, hurt and hinder us, but God will only do so because He knows that He will use the devil's schemes for our eventual benefit.

So, if you are down and feel that life is completely unbearable, remember: you may be sad because of something you did, or because of some chemical imbalance, or because something terrible has happened in your life, but your sadness is always an opportunity for God to make you a better person.

Depression will always hurt and it will always be around, but it is fantastic to know that the Comforter, the Holy Spirit, has promised to console us in our grief and sustain us through our dark days.

CHAPTER 10:

Under the Magnifying Glass

My home state of Oregon is known for its rain. Actually, it's known for being mispronounced as "Or-ee-gone," when it is, in fact, pronounced "Organ." Anyway, there are, perhaps, four months in the summer when it will be sunny. One summer, Young Ken decided it would be fun to take out his Junior Sleuth magnifying glass and fry some ants. Only in later years did I learn that this was considered to be socially unacceptable behavior in Oregon and everywhere on the West Coast…go figure.

Anyway, I went through a pyromaniac phase where I would use my magnifying glass to harness the sun's power to set things on fire. It was the coolest thing ever! Even today, I love to watch a bonfire blaze and will gaze into the scintillating display of color and raw power until my eyes start to glaze over and the hair on my legs starts to singe off from the proximity to the inferno.

As Christians, we sometimes feel like we are under the magnifying glass. Not just being examined, but being fried. On a personal scale, we feel the eyes of our friends, family, and coworkers boring holes into our backs, waiting for us to fall. Corporately, as a Christian body, we feel the crush of the media and the machinations of the politicians, both of whom try to make it a bit more difficult for us to love our enemies and pray for our persecutors. They want to watch us fail and fall. Few are they that cheer when we succeed, but many are they that cheer when we fail.

Cool.

I know this book focuses a lot on trials, tribulations, and jerks picking on you, but, frankly, the Bible talks a lot about this topic, too. It's important because we, as humans, tend to like to be liked and it can be very painful when those around you are staring intently at you, waiting to see if your fly is down so they may feel justified in pointing and laughing.

Therefore, this segment is not a bit about trying to encourage you because you are being scrutinized, but is rather a cautionary chapter to not break under the strain.

The constant pressure of constant surveillance is sure to cause people to crack. It always does. We see it when we watch movie stars crack under the strain of being popular. We see it in our politicians, when men who started out trying to do the right thing begin to court prostitutes or take bribes. We Christians, however, run the risk of cracking under the strain of holding unpopular and "intolerant" beliefs in a world that insists that their own morality be accepted and celebrated. We run the risk of compromise.

It is interesting to see how many groups out there are trying to get acceptance from us, the Christians, even if they will not acknowledge that they care what we think. Advocacy groups for homosexuals are constantly trying to win us over to their side, to welcome their lifestyle with open arms. Our friends want us to accept their choices because they know us personally and care about our approval. Our family, most of all, wants us to look at them and say that we are proud of what they are doing. Everyone wants to be accepted, and since Christians have high standards, people try to convince us to bring those standards down a little bit so that they may be recognized by us.

It becomes very easy for us to say "I'm a Christian; I shouldn't care about what other's think of me. I only need God's approval." Yeah, that's true, but a good reputation is better than gold or silver. Or Xbox 360s, or Ferraris, or Rolexes. Therefore, we should be like Daniel.

Daniel was a Hebrew prince who had been taken captive and sent to Babylon in slavery. While there, he impressed a steady line of succession of Babylonian and Persian kings. All the while, he maintained his devotion to God, even when he was promoted to a position of great power.

His rapid rise to power got the people around him jealous. The other rulers of the Persian Empire looked at Daniel and tried to find some misdeed to accuse him of. Why should this Hebrew be of greater power than true-blood Persians? They scrutinized his every action to see if he, a royal hostage, would speak against the Persian king, Darius, or would subtly rebel and break any of his laws.

Despite their best efforts to find fault with Daniel, they could not find a single infraction to hang around his neck. Therefore, they concocted a ruse to make his religious observance illegal. You know the rest: Daniel was thrown into a lions' den, was protected by God so that the lions didn't touch him, and then the people that accused him were tossed into the den and the lions ripped them to shreds.

We see from Daniel the perfect example of how Christians (albeit, Daniel was 500 years before Christ) are supposed to live: so blamelessly and without fault that people have to make up accusations against you. Jesus said on the Sermon on the Mount, "Blessed are you when they revile and persecute you and say all kinds of evil against you falsely for My sake."

Everywhere around us, people are watching us. We are lights in a world of darkness, and people want to see that light glow a little dimmer so that their deeds may continue to be unexamined and will no longer be scrutinized by people who claim to have an objective moral code.

Be wary if you think you stand, because it is very easy to let pride puff you up and make your fall all the more painful. And everyone is wanting you to fall.

CHAPTER 11:

Maturing Like Wine Instead of Like Cheese

When I was a boy, I had a very clear sense of what was right and what was wrong. Now, logically and biblically speaking, I was not always correct in what I judged to be good or bad, but I did not doubt that I was right. In my mind, the world was composed of blacks and whites. There was no room for grey because my understanding was not tainted by cynicism, or the experience that comes with age. All I saw I passed through the filter of what I had been taught was good and proper behavior.

Now that I have aged, I have come to see the world through a slightly different pair of glasses and can see a variety of colors of morality as I look at things like "extenuating circumstances," or think that something I once held as vital and important was now juvenile and immature thinking. I have been told that as I get older, this tendency will increase as right and wrong will become more jumbled and the line of moral absolutes become more blurred as life makes me more cynical or "wise," if you prefer.

All kids see life in absolutes and it is only through exposure to the adult world that we learn compromise and grey areas and little white lies. It is only through exposure to those older than us that we learn how to "mature" to be like them.

I think wisdom is called for here. In the Bible, we see that the Law – the standard of right and wrong, good and bad – was established as a tutor to instruct us in the way we must go and to provide us with an objective standard to live by. The Mosaic Law was often harsh because it had to be. God was creating a society that was different from those around it and was trying to shield His people from things that would harm them.

For example, God told the children of Israel that they could not eat pork. Nowadays, pork is a staple in many people's diet. Most Americans love bacon, find ham to be a tasty Easter tradition, and enjoy the savory flavor of pork chops. Our pigs are usually fed on grain and, when cooked, are cooked so that the potential dangers of trichinosis are eliminated. It seems unfair to us that God would restrict the Israelites from such a tasty meal.

However, in the ancient times, pigs were fed anything and everything and were often plagued with bacteria and viruses. Since it was difficult to cook pork to an exact 160 degrees Fahrenheit, people would often contract trichinosis - a parasite that has the potential of inflicting serious damage on the central nervous system. So, while the ancient world was dying from the food they were eating, the Israelites, if obedient to the dietary strictures of the Law, would live longer, healthier lives.

When Jesus came, He said specifically that He did not come to remove one dot of an "i" or cross of a "t" of the Law, but through Him, the purpose of the Law is fulfilled. The tutor ceased to have the role of authority over us and becomes a guide and an example of how gracious God is to us.

The Law's purpose, to show us that we cannot fulfill the standard of God's perfection, has been fulfilled, and we can now be led by the hand, by the Law to Jesus. Now, we live in the new covenant, whose conditions are laid out for us in the prophecies of Jeremiah, chapter 31, verses 31-34:

"Behold, the days are coming," says the LORD, "when I will make a new covenant with the house of Israel and with the house of Judah – not according to the covenant that I made with their fathers in the day that I took them by the hand to lead them out of the land of Egypt, My covenant which they broke, though I was a husband to them, says the LORD. I will put my law in their minds, and write it on their hearts; and I will be their God and they shall be my people. No more shall every man teach his neighbor and every man his brother, saying, 'Know the LORD,' for they all shall know Me, from the least of them to the greatest of them, says the LORD. For I will forgive their iniquity and their sin will I remember no more."

In this New Covenant, we no longer need a priest or a pastor to tell us how to live, because we hear the Holy Spirit speaking directly to our hearts, whispering to us, comforting us, encouraging us. He stands by us in our weakness and triumphs with us in our strengths. It is He that teaches us how to praise properly and it is He that emboldens us to declare the name of Christ to the lost. The New Covenant is not about legalism; a system of laws designed to weigh a man down, frightening him with his own inadequacies. Rather, the New Covenant is like having a hands-free Bluetooth and on the other end, the Holy Spirit is whispering to us how to act and behave, and telling us that we are loved, even in our failures.

So how does the New Covenant and the work of the Holy Spirit coincide with right and wrong? Simple. Today's Christians do not listen to the Holy Spirit and we do not keep the terms of the New Covenant. Like the Israelites of old, we are stiff-necked individuals, insisting on our own ways and our own paths. We are like some old dog, incapable of hearing, too tired to get up, and too lazy to move beyond our comfortable spot in front of the fireplace. We have become old Christians, weary and set in our ways. We choose to ignore the voice of the Holy Spirit, hoping that He will just go away and leave us be.

We do not listen to Him telling us right from wrong and we do not hear Him tell us when and where He wants us to go. As we "mature," we do not mature like fine wine, but rather become like a rotten block of cheese: smelly, hard, and covered in fungus. Even though the Law was established as a tutor, there is still that standard of right and wrong that the Holy Spirit established in us and it is to that standard we must return. The Law still protects us from sin that would harm us, if we allow it to.

Therefore, I propose that the truly mature Christian does not forget the black and white morality of the child. I propose that she knows right from wrong and knows the will of God because she is constantly listening to the Holy Spirit. She is not cynical from years of experience because she has not allowed the troubles of this life to pierce her inner serenity that only comes from a right relationship with God. Calluses of the heart must be rubbed away for the Christian to become mature to the point of childlike faith. It is only the immature that insist on coming to God on their own terms rather than running to Him like a child running to her Daddy.

That is how a mature Christian looks. In faith and in standards of morality, the Christian is a child; looking with eager anticipation to what their Daddy says is right and wrong, and believing that He is right simply because of who He is. Someday, I hope that I have this kind of faith and that my moral standards are so high that I can be a child.

CHAPTER 12:

Born With Purpose

"For I know the thoughts that I think toward you, says the Lord, thoughts of peace and not of evil, to give you a future and a hope." Jeremiah 29:11

I went to a Christian school when I was growing up. We always had a chapel every Monday or Wednesday (it changed every so often). We would have pastors and motivational speakers come in and tell us God's will for our lives.

This is very good, because teens and young adults should be instructed from an early age as to how they can come to know God.

Unfortunately, some of these men were snake-oil salesmen, peddling to us a gospel of "purpose." We could be assured of leading a more fulfilled existence if we only knew our purpose in life. If we only knew that God has BIG plans for us, then we can be content in our high self esteem and go out and be somebody!

This is a milquetoast gospel. Have you ever eaten milquetoast? First you soak bread in milk, then you eat it, and then you vomit it back up because it tastes terrible.

Some of these motivational speakers used verses like the one at the beginning of the chapter to let the reader know that God cares about them. That's nice. That's a little warm fuzzy that I am going to cuddle up to when I go to bed tonight. Maybe it will give me good dreams. Oh. But I should probably read a couple of verses before and after that verse, just to make sure I get the right picture. Make SURE I understand what God was saying rather than just assume that He was saying that He wanted a better life for me.

God – through Jeremiah – was encouraging a bunch of refugees in Babylon. He (God) told the refugees that they should be content where they were at; make a life for themselves, but be ready to return, because He was going to release them to return to Israel. Then God goes on to deliver a very famous, powerful, and touching promise to His children:

"For thus says the Lord: After seventy years are completed in Babylon, I will visit you and perform My good word toward you, and cause you to return to this place. For I know the thoughts that I think toward you, says the Lord, thoughts of peace and not of evil, to give you a future and a hope. Then you will call upon Me and go and pray to me, and I will listen to you. And you will seek Me and find Me when you search for me with all your heart. I will be found by you, says the Lord, and I will bring you back from your captivity; I will gather you from all the nations and from all the places where I have driven you, says the Lord, and I will bring you to the place from which I cause you to be carried away captive (Jer. 29:10-15)."

Judah was desperate and destitute. They had failed to listen to the prophets and God had done exactly what He said He would do; He sent Babylon several times to punish the nation of Judah, and each time, Babylon killed many and took others captive. Those that were captive in this foreign land must have been terrified. They must have felt that God was finished with them. That He had thrown in the cosmic towel and wiped His hands of them.

But no. God – through Jeremiah – tells these captives that He will keep His promises and will bring them back to Jerusalem and back to Judah and back to Israel. Not only that, but He reassures them by saying, "Guys, you blew it, and you know that you failed. I may be punishing you now, but I want you to know that I love you; I don't hate you. I have plans for you. I have plans on this scale: there will come a day when you will want to know Me and you will seek for Me, and I will make Myself known to you, because I want you to know Me."

Where is the application in this set of verses for us? It's not in finding a purpose for our lives. Instead, to me, this verse is about realizing that God does not hate us when we are going through those difficult spots in our lives. Guys, life's hard. You already know this and you don't need me to tell you that life can be brutal. God did not sugarcoat it for us at the Garden of Eden. He said we'd have to eke out an existence through the sweat on our backs and He was right. Jesus took it a step further by telling His followers that their lives would be even more difficult than that of the ordinary man as they would suffer persecution for preaching Christ.

When we are afflicted by the burdens of life, we may feel discouraged. We may feel that God hates us. Like Job, we may curse the day we were born and wish that we had died in our mother's womb. But. (there's always a "but," isn't there?) But God would not have us think this way. He does not think evil towards us. He is not plotting in Heaven saying, "You know what, I am really tired of that Ken Dickason. I think…yes, I think I will send the IRS to audit him this year, just for kicks." He doesn't get bored and decide to spice things up by causing trouble for us. He allows us to endure trials that He knows we can handle so that we will love Him more as we come to depend on Him and spend time praying and talking to Him, becoming acclimated to His will.

As for your purpose in life? That is the simplest thing in the world. I'll give you two verses that sum up EVERYTHING that you need to be to live your own directive-guided existence.

The first comes to us from King Solomon. In the book of Ecclesiastes, Solomon describes his life as a pursuit of meaning. He tried to find satisfaction through women, drink, intelligence, hard work, but in the end he found that all his efforts were meaningless. He could not find any purpose or value in pursuing the things that we normally consider, "good," or what the Bible calls sin. Instead, he says this: "Let us hear the conclusion of the whole matter [his search to find meaning to life]: Fear God and keep His commandments, for this is man's all. For God will bring every work into judgment, including every secret thing, whether good or evil."

Simple. Straightforward. Man's purpose is boiled down into one sentence.

Solomon's admonition carries both a warning and a promise. He says that man's purpose is to serve God – in whatever capacity God has declared for that man – and obey His commandments, BECAUSE God will make known everything that we have ever done. This is a warning because those dirty, little thoughts of ours will be made public before Christ. We must harness our tongue, because, as the Bible says, every idle word will be subject to judgment. We are responsible for our actions. The buck literally stops with us.

However, there is a promise hidden in this passage: "every secret thing, whether good or evil." Jesus told us to do good in secret so that our Father, who rewards in secret, will see our good deeds and be pleased. Therefore, not only will our hidden sins be revealed, but all the things we did secretly for the benefit of others. When you got that bonus check and you gave 20% tithe instead of 10%; God saw that. When you spent time teaching baseball to a boy who has no father, God saw that, too. God is not sitting up in Heaven hoping that you will stumble so that He may zap you. He is, in fact, waiting to reward you.

In the book of Revelation, Jesus says that He is coming soon and that He is bringing His rewards with Him. Why would He say this if not to encourage us? He didn't say, "I'm coming back. The earth better be in tip-top shape when I return," or, "I'm coming back, and this time, I am so mad at you Christians." He said He is coming, coming soon, and we should be ready. Like Israel, we are told to live and plan for tomorrow and a hundred years from now, but to prepare ourselves for the time when we will be released from captivity in our own Babylon, because release could come at any moment...maybe... even...now...

The other verse I have for you comes from Jesus and tells you what it means, as a Christian, to fear God and keep His commandments: "Go therefore and make disciples of all the nations, baptizing them in the name of the Father and of the Son and of the Holy Spirit, teaching them to observe all things that I have commanded you; and lo, I am with you always, even to the end of the age."

These are our two directives; the purpose that we can find for our lives. As I read the Bible, I can find no simpler explanation for how a man should live his life and how a Christian should live out his Christianity. Actually, perhaps there is an even simpler verse for us: "You shall love the LORD your God with all your heart, with all your soul, and with all your mind," and "You shall love your neighbor as yourself." Everything else – your entire purpose – can be summed into the three passages that I have pointed you to. Everything else is just gravy.

CHAPTER 13:

The Church and Politics; Strange Bedfellows

Every so often we hear from the pulpit that we Christians are to be the salt of the world and the light in a dark room. The pastor then draws some kind of artful analogy between this verse and the current political climate, whatever that may be at the time. It seems to be a way for the pastor to say, "If you vote for such-and-such and pass so-and-so a bill, the world will be better off and Christianity will have an easier time of it. And God will like you better if you vote conservative and hate you if you vote liberal. And God just <u>hates</u> taxes."

"Salt and light of the world." This can't be implying that Christians should ensure that the political climate is favorable to Christianity because the political climate has <u>never</u> been favorable to biblical Christianity. Early Church? Killed for being saved. Constantinian era? The "political climate" was summed up in a decree by the emperor that made everyone in the empire a "Christian," thus incorporating a bunch of pagan beliefs that we're still trying to get rid of. In the Middle Ages, the political climate was to keep the public from reading the Bible by putting it in a language they did not understand. During the Reformation, Protestants were killed by Catholics and Catholics were killed by Protestants. In England, for many years, the "Church of England" was like saying "Catholic-lite," and they still killed people for being of a different religion. America allowed for some religious freedom, but it was not built by Christian principles, as we so want to believe.

If Jesus had wanted us to be politicians, He'd have had the apostles become senators in Rome (or, at least, Paul, since he was a Roman citizen). Why didn't Paul become a senator? He could have had ample opportunity to talk about Jesus to thousands and could have brought reform to the empire. I suggest that the reason (other than the obvious "he wasn't called to") is because it would have killed him. Another obvious answer? Sort of, but there is a deeper meaning hidden in that statement.

You see, politics kills Christianity. Separation between church and state is in place, not because Christianity has no place in politics, but because politics corrupts, waters down, and kills the faith of the believer.

"But Ken, what about the Founding Fathers?" Most of them weren't Christians. Several of them believed that there probably was a God. A couple of them believed in God, believed in Jesus, but did not believe that Jesus was God, and therefore did not have the power to save us from our sins. I have no doubt that George Washington was a Christian. A few others throughout the years have probably been Christians, but look at what politics has done to otherwise strong Christians. Instead of being remembered as a man of God, George Washington is remembered as the Father of our Country. I think that might make him sad, even though he would probably be proud of the fact that the country has lasted this long.

Politics corrupts Christians as it corrupts anyone. It makes us compromise what should not be compromised. Either we abandon our sense of right and wrong in order to please others, or we abandon our love for others in order to push our agenda for what is right and wrong. It's why men like Jerry Falwell and Pat Robertson experienced such limited success in the political arena. People saw that, really, theirs' was not the loving Christianity of the Bible, but the Christianity of social agenda and political reform.

Social reform suggests a certain political inclination, and there is always the question as to what side of an issue Jesus would be on, but even more often, many have asked, "Would Jesus have been a conservative or a liberal?" I suggest that He'd have been neither. A conservative strives for a preservation of the established way at the exclusion of newer ideas, while a liberal's goal is to throw out old-fashioned ideals in favor of that which is new. For Jesus to have been either, He would have had to have been in support of or opposed to either upholding the Mosaic Law as it was or of abolishing it totally. He did neither. He said that He had not come to destroy the Law, but fulfill it. He became the first libertarian by upholding the Old Law by giving us a new understanding (ironically, the 'new' understanding was the original intent all along). He showed us love. "Love the Lord your God...[and]...love your neighbor as yourself." He summed up all 400+ laws of the Old Testament into two laws, which is, in reality, only one: the law of love.

In other words, Jesus did not tell us to follow the old Law or give us a set of new laws to follow, but instead showed us the freedom that lies in grace. Therefore, I believe that, were Jesus to be given a political ideology, He would be a libertarian. Of course, you shouldn't take that TOO seriously and assume that Jesus would have towed the libertarian party line. Just because He seemed to fall more into that category does not mean that He would approve of all that being a libertarian entails (for example, libertarians tend to prefer near-anarchy and overthrow of corrupt governments. Jesus did not).

Now, allegories aside, we need to take a serious look at our participation in the political process based on the Early Church's involvement in politics (read: none) and the principles that Jesus set down for us.

First of all (and perhaps most importantly), is to observe obedience for the government in which you are a part. Whether you are an American and think the ACLU is ruining the nation, or in Communist China where the government is ruining the nation, or in Iran, where the people that are ruining the nation will also kill you.

In the book of Romans, Paul told a persecuted group of believers (in the heart of Rome) to respect the governing authorities as the authority that God has placed over them. In fact, he goes so far as to say "Let every soul be subject to the governing authorities. For there is no authority except from God and appointed by God. Therefore whoever resists the authority resists the ordinance of God, and those who resist will bring judgment on themselves."

I don't know about you, but I do not read any room for rebellion against even a corrupt government. When Paul was writing this letter, Caesar Nero was in power. Nero was nuts. He would dip Christians in tar, light them on fire, and use them as human candles in his gardens. He would…well, I don't really want to appeal to our baser instincts by saying all that Nero did, so let's just say that he was a horrible man that did many horrible things. You can probably google Nero to get more information.

If Paul were ever going to tell Christians that it was ok to rebel against their government, it would have been under the reign of Caesar Nero. However, if he had done that, Christianity would have become a legitimate enemy of the state and the Romans were very good at quashing rebellions and insurrections. As it was, when the Christians were thrown to the lions, they did not curse their accusers and did not renounce their faith. Thousands upon thousands of people died, but even more people came to the faith because of the testimony of those that counted it an honor and a glory to be worthy of dying for Christ. The Romans, who were so enamored with honor and glory, that they said, "These Christians die well."

Are Paul's words not good enough for you? Let's go a bit further back to the life of Jesus. In Jesus' last week before the Cross, we read that the Pharisees, wanting to trap Jesus, asked him if it were lawful to pay taxes to Caesar, a pagan king. If Jesus had answered that it was lawful, then He would anger the Jewish people, who chaffed under Roman oppression. If He said that it was not lawful, then He would be arrested for treason and insurrection.

Knowing the trap, Jesus says to the Pharisees: "Render to Caesar the things that are Caesar's and to God the things that are God's (Matthew 22:15-22)." In other words, Jesus was saying to respect the authority of the government insomuch as it does not violate giving God His due, for God has precedence.

Even further back to the book of 1st Samuel, chapter 24: the life of David. At this point David is being pursued by the near-maniacal King Saul, who has made several threats against David's life and is pursuing David across the countryside in an attempt for Saul to save face by killing David.

Saul's chase against David diverted the nation's military from patrolling and guarding its borders to pursuing David. People were dying because Saul wanted to kill David to salve his own pride.

At one point in the chase, Saul went into a cave to...well...relieve himself. Turns out, this cave was one of David's strongholds. David sees Saul, answering the call of nature, and the men with David tried to persuade David to kill Saul. Rather than kill him, David sneaks up on Saul and cuts a corner from his robe. Immediately he feels guilty because he acted in violence against the Lord's anointed. David then calls out to Saul and tells the king that he could have killed him, but God did not want David to, so he did not.

The point is, from a secular point of view, David had every right to kill King Saul who was not only trying to kill David, but was hurting his nation by diverting precious resources into the chase of a man the king hated. However, David knew that God had made Saul king and it would not be right to kill him, even though Saul was a bad king.

Kinda cuts you to the quick, doesn't it? We Americans are rebellious by nature. Probably comes from the roots of how this nation was founded. However, our rebelliousness, our hatred for "The Man" is not biblical and is, if the Bible is to be believed (it is), actually rebellion against God.

I'm going to say something that I have never heard in any sermon or read in any book, so it may not be true. Take what I have said about authority, cross reference it with the Bible, and then apply it to the following statement: if the Founders of our country were really Christians, then in rebelling against the British Empire, they were acting in an unchristian-like manner, which negates our claim that this country was founded on Christian values. Our nation was founded on rebellion. We can say it was founded on liberty and the proposition of equality if that will assuage our consciences, but in reality, our country was founded on the unbiblical rebellion of people against a lawful, God-appointed government.

That's probably unpatriotic for me to say that. I can accept that. Likewise, it was unchristian when the Christian Right rebelled against President Clinton, and it was unchristian when many Christians mocked Bush, and it is now unchristian for Christians to mock President Obama and to hate Congress for...well, whatever mess Congress is involved in at the moment; to disrespect the authority that God has given him over us is to disrespect God (Romans 13:2).

Now, we have all seen the war movies where the young rebel private has to deal with a curmudgeonly lieutenant and we hear the phrase, "We salute the rank, Private. Not the man." Yeah. I can see that as fitting. The Christians in the Early Church were certainly not in a position to think that Nero was a paragon of virtue or an exemplar of leadership. The distinction needs to be made between liking and revering the man and respecting the fact that God gave him authority over us.

It may also be important to look at Jesus' teachings about government. I have recently talked to some friends that believed that everything Jesus preached – such as turning the other cheek, and loving your enemies – should apply to governments and heads of state as well. To do so is to take Jesus out of context and to misunderstand the role that God has given the heads of state: to protect and defend the people that are governed. In fact, the very first mandate that God gave the government was the right to administer the death penalty as a means of exacting justice (Genesis 9:5-6). Therefore, any government that gives up the execution of heinous criminals is giving up their right to be called a government that protects its people and provides justice to the masses.

No, if you are looking for advice for rulers, the best place to look is the book of Proverbs and Ecclesiastes. Seriously, both books were written by King Solomon – with contributions from other wise men – and were originally intended as advice for kings. Solomon addresses many of his proverbs to his children, who would rule after he died. If a president were to read Proverbs, then he would have a solid basis for a government, but reading the teachings of Jesus – while showing him what a Christian should be like – would not create a strong foundation for a nation because Jesus was not directing His words to a state entity, but towards the hearts and minds of individuals who had to live their lives in a world that would hate them.

We are to be lights in this world, reflecting the brilliance of Christ into the darkness, to expose evil for what it is, but we are then to lead people out of that darkness rather than condemning them for being in it. In other words, it is not our place to make our lives about social reform, or about stopping the gay marriage bills. Rather, as Christians, we are to act intelligently; affect our surroundings; change the tide of politics if we can, but never lose sight of the fact that our true calling; the Divine Mandate, is to love others and then show them that Jesus wants to free them from their sin.

CHAPTER 14:

Witnessing

A book about Christianity would not be complete without the author offering his $.02 about witnessing. Pretty much everyone agrees that Christians should witness. I mean, Jesus told us that we are 1). The light of the World (Matt 5:14), 2). The only hope for some people to hear about Jesus (Rom 10:14), 3). God's ambassadors (2 Cor. 5:20). The only thing that is not told to us is how to witness, and that should raise several flags of curiosity in our minds.

Earlier in this book, in the chapter on love, I explain the importance of witnessing, so it would be redundant to explain that to witness to a person is perhaps the greatest expression of love that we can offer them. I will, however, go on to explain the "why" of witnessing and offer some advice into the "how" of witnessing (as in all things, if the Bible does not explicitly state something, it is up to the individual to use their God-given minds to reason out what might or might not be true, and then prayerfully form their own opinion).

Back to the "why." It is easy for me to say, "Witness! Because Jesus *told* you to!" but that won't satisfy your intellectual curiosity. Besides, I know that whenever I am told, "Do this!" without being told why, I do the exact opposite.

First of all, let me state that there are dozens of verses that I could use for this section. All over the Old and New Testament, Christians (or, in the Old Testament, Jews) are told to tell others of the glory of God. I chose these three verses (Matt 5:14, Rom 10:14, 2 Cor. 5:20) because I find them to both provide intriguing analogies between witnessing and temporal experiences - such as the light of a candle, or the representation of an ambassador - and because I find the arguments that each verse presents to be compelling.

Now. The "light of the world." The exact verse says "You are the light of the world. A city that is set on a hill cannot be hidden." Have you ever gone into a dark room and flicked on a light switch? You notice that – unless the light bulb is burned out – the light pierces the darkness and you find that the room is bright, for darkness vanishes in the presence of light. All that was in the room is exposed and laid bare for the eye to see and the person may now get to work. In the same sense, Christians are supposed to lighten the areas they are in, lovingly expose sin, and show people Jesus so that they may live for His glory.

However, the analogy continues in Matthew chapter 5 as Jesus goes on to say "Nor do they light a lamp and put it under a basket, but on a lampstand, and it gives light to all who are in the house." You do not buy a $50 lamp at Bed, Bath, & Beyond and then neglect to turn it on. That would be a waste of money. You purchased the lamp to brighten your house. In the same way, Christians were not redeemed from our sins so that we could cloister ourselves in a hideaway, waiting for Jesus to come back and smite the unbelievers. We were saved from sin so that we might go out and multiply by showing people Jesus and then lead them to Him. To bring "The Light" to the "darkness" of sin.

Our second verse touches on the desperation and the importance of witnessing. In discussing that everyone who calls on the Lord will be saved, Paul asks the rhetorical question, "How then shall they [unbelievers] call on Him in whom they have not believed? And how shall they believe in Him of whom they have not heard? And how shall they hear without a preacher?"

In other words:

Point A: A person needs to trust in Jesus to be saved.

Point B: They cannot trust a person in whom they have not believed.

Point C: They cannot believe in a person that they have not heard of.

Point D: They will never hear of Him unless someone tells them about Him.

This isn't a call for you to go to Africa and talk to the Bushmen (although, if God is telling you to do that, you'd better get off your duff and go talk to the Bushmen), rather, this is a call for you to look around you and realize that many (majority?) of those around you have never heard of the Real Jesus. I use the word "Real" because the media and academia has portrayed a Jesus that does not really exist. Their Jesus is either overly judgmental and does not love the sinner or the sin, or He is too loving and does not care about the sin.

These are neutered "Jesuses" and neither can save a person because neither actually exist. They are parodies or mockeries of the original and can only be propaganda disseminated by the Enemy.

The point of witnessing is to preach a real, biblical representation of sin and grace and to present Jesus for who He really is to anyone that the Holy Spirit is leading you to talk to, and show the nonbeliever that Jesus loves them and wants to save them from their sin and wants them to know Him.

Our final verse addresses our positions as witnesses for Jesus. We are ambassadors of God. What is an ambassador? He is a representative of the sovereignty of a foreign nation to another nation. In theory, he is supposed to discuss the desires of the leaders of his own nation with the leaders of the nation in which he is stationed. In this situation, we are the ambassadors, the mouthpieces of God, "as though God were pleading through us." In theory, ambassadors should be treated with respect, lest they incur the wrath of the other sovereign nation. In our case, however, we are not respected ambassadors. We are hated by the World. We represent an unpopular Sovereign who lives in a far-off nation, so it is not unusual for the World to hate and revile and kill us.

This shouldn't be surprising since Jesus said that that was how things were supposed to happen. If the world hated Him, they should, by association, hate His mouthpieces.

But you should know the type of person that hates Jesus. It is not the man that realizes he is a sinner or the woman that knows she is unclean. The person that hates Jesus is the man who thinks he has everything together. That he does not need a Savior and can get to God on his own steam. In Jesus' case, it was the Pharisees, Sadducees and the Scribes. In our case...well, it can be anyone that thinks that they are "good enough" and are not interested in what Jesus has to offer.

How are we supposed to witness to an entire world that hates us and the King we represent? We get the whole gamut of ways to minister from the book of Acts. We see great evangelists like Peter and Paul talking to whole crowds of people that they do not know. We see men like Philip, who were led to talk to a specific person at a specific time. We see men that work by miracles and we see men that win people over by the "foolishness of Christ." We see women like Dorcas who simply ministered to people and loved them.

There are whole books and series of books written about how you can and should witness. I think the simplest (and most accurate) answer is to say, "listen to the Holy Spirit." If He is telling you to talk to your parents who have rejected God their entire lives, then you'd better do it. If He is telling you to go up to some person that you've never met and ask them about their perspective on eternity, then you'd better do it.

It is important to have a good understanding of the Bible before you start so that you can answer any questions that come up, but if you are a new Christian who is still learning, do not think that you cannot still witness. Sometimes, the most compelling evidence for a person is to see how Christ has "made...[you] a new creation." I am convinced that there is no cookie-cutter method for witnessing to people because I have seen the most bizarre and unique methods bear fruit. When I was in college I saw those "crazy" people that stand on their soap boxes gain converts for Christ; I saw the "quiet" witness bring someone to Jesus; and I witnessed people getting saved over internet chat rooms.

Therefore, if God can work through any method and through anybody, I would strongly urge you to be careful before you stop a person from witnessing in a way that you find "too extreme." Unless they are going out of their way to make the gospel of Christ more offensive than it already is (yelling in people's faces, cussing, being unbiblical, etc), then I would advise you just send up a silent prayer that he/she is following God's directions and that His will be done. By doing this, you may help that radical more than if you were to go and offer him advice or condemn him for his efforts. Of course, if an evangelist is going overboard, then prayerfully consider talking to him; it may very well be that this person has let his own agenda creep in and is no longer obeying.

Remember, we may not all be called to be evangelists, but we are all called to "be ready to give a defense to everyone who asks you a reason for the hope that is in you, with meekness and fear (1 Peter 3:15)."

We are all lights, we are all ministers of grace, and we are all ambassadors of our King. Let's act like it.

CHAPTER 15:

Prayer

In the three years that He actively preached, Jesus talked about a lot of different things. Mainly He talked about our conduct towards man and our conduct towards God. He may not have spent much time talking about prayer, but we see from His personal life that prayer was a vital factor in how He got through every day. His example sets the example that we are to live by, and since He was in constant communication with His Father, so should we be.

In today's society, prayer is one of the most book-heavy subjects because, frankly, most of us don't know how to do it. There are only a few examples of prayer in the New Testament. Most prayers come to us from the Old Testament, and a lot of people think that we should disregard everything in the Old Testament because it is "old."

Well, with that logic, let's ignore people over the age of fifty because, let's face it, they're on the downhill slope. We might as well kill them by sixty, because, with the previously stated logic, they would be of no more practical use to anyone (even themselves) by the time they're this old.

Don't euthanize your old people and don't euthanize your Old Testament. Both are wellsprings of knowledge which we are blessed to be able to enjoy and learn from.

Back to prayer. Prayer is one of the best ways we Christians have to communicate with God, but some opportunistic individuals have used the topic of prayer to mislead others. Some people have the audacity to claim that prayer is your way of getting what you want from God. They mishandle the words of Jesus: "and whatever things you ask, in prayer, believing, you shall receive."

If a person prays, thinking that God will give them whatever they want, then they have a very limited perception of who God is because they seem to believe that He is nothing more than a genie in a bottle. "God, yesterday You gave me a Ferrari, and that was nice, but today, I want a Lamborghini." Or, an even more popular derivation of this type of prayer is the belief that you can get anything you want, as long as it sounds spiritual. "God, I really want you to save [insert name here] so that I can marry him/her."

I'm pretty sure that God does not look too favorably on these selfish requests. Oddly enough, I have read a book where a man encouraged us to pray selfishly for God's kingdom to be advanced on the earth and so that we can benefit from that spreading, or something like that. Never, ever, EVER has God, Jesus, the apostles, the epistle writers, the prophets, the psalmists, Solomon, or the historians told us to be selfish with God in ANY WAY.

To be selfish with God is to be sacrilegious, disrespectful, and is blatantly stupid. To do so is to completely disregard His sovereignty. Why do I say this? Because the selfish prayer does not ask "God, Your will be done," but demands "God, My will be done."

The people that want us to be selfish say that we have been given permission to come boldly before the throne of grace, which means that we have the opportunity to be bold in the American manner. Allow me to elaborate.

Let's take a little trip down memory lane to the book of Esther. Esther was made the Queen of the Persian Empire. She had great favor before the king, Xerxes, but when she had to come before him and ask a favor of him, she feared for her life, because boldness before the king was a death warrant. So, she prayed and fasted fervently, went before the king, and he did not kill her, but instead welcomed her into his presence.

Therefore, I propose that when we Christians are told to come boldly before the throne of grace, we are not to come sauntering down the hall, kicking God's servants out of the way, stand before His throne and demand that He acquiesce to us. Rather, we Christians are to not fear to bring any request to Him because He is not going to kill us dead for asking from Him. He loves us and wants to spend time with us, so He wants us to pray. How can the two of us be friends if I am unable to talk to Him for fear of offending Him?

There is to be a balance between the friendly familiarity that a son has with his Father, and the respect that one has for his King.

When it came to prayer, Jesus gave the crowds at the Mount of Olives one example, but His prayer was so unusual, that the apostles went to Him privately and asked Him to repeat it, because it was confusing to them how easily one might pray to God.

Perhaps they thought that Jesus would share some special insight with them that He did not tell the crowds. Instead, He shortened the prayer that He had said the first time and told them, "When you pray, say 'Our Father in heaven, hallowed be Your name. Your kingdom come. Your will be done on earth as it is in heaven. Give us day by day our daily bread, and forgive us our sins, for we also forgive everyone who is indebted to us. And do not lead us into temptation, but deliver us from the evil one.'"

He did not say "repeat this short verse from an obscure passage from scripture if you want to be blessed," or "You know what, guys? Just ask Me for whatever you want. I'm making a list, and I want to make sure I get you the good stuff because, as we all know, you only go around once." No. Jesus gave His disciples a very simple (not simplistic) model for them to follow.

So that you can get the context, Jesus goes on to explain the principles of prayer to the apostles. Through the use of parables, Jesus says that God wants us to pray persistently, not giving up when we think God is not answering us, because Jesus promises that God will give good gifts to His children (us).

Now that raises an interesting question that many pastors - who were really wolves in sheep's skins - have used to tell people a Gospel of prosperity. If you are not healthy, wealthy, and glad, it is because you have not been asking God for the good things in life.

These pastors lead people astray by their translation of this verse, because who is to determine what "good" is? Us? Certainly not! When Jesus gave the analogy of God giving good gifts, He said that when a child asks for bread, a father would not give him a stone. But children often ask for ridiculous things. I asked my parents for video game system from the day I was 5 years old. My parents knew better, though. They knew that I would only play that video game and would never interact with other people my age. I would grow fat and ugly and become socially distant. So they waited until they felt I was ready and then gave me a Nintendo 64, which, at the time, was the best a kid could get. I was very happy that day.

Similarly, we can ask God for things that He knows we are not yet ready for. We can ask for a relationship that we cannot cope with, we ask for a job that would overwhelm us, we ask for a car that would encourage us to speed too fast so that we'd die in a blazing inferno. God knows what is best for us and He does not give out gifts blindly. He will give as He wants to. He will give according to His will.

James, the half-brother of Jesus, once wrote, "Where do wars and fights come from among you? Do they not come from your desires for pleasure that war in your members? ...yet you do not have because you do not ask. You ask and do not receive, because you ask amiss that you may spend it on your pleasures (James 4:1-3)." James had prosperity ministers in his day, too. Christians who thought that God existed to do our will rather than the other way around.

Maybe it's best to put this a different way: God will do whatever He wants. And that's just the way it is. Period. Therefore, I suppose the point of prayer is for us humans to try to divine the Divine Will. How best to know what God wants from us then to ask Him? When we ask Him for such-and-such, we are letting Him know what we want and we give Him an opportunity to tell us, "No, Kenny. I'm not giving you that fancy job that pays $50,000 a year. I've got something better for you."

Therefore, my advice to you (and I'd advise you to check me on this in your Bible) is to pray, expecting God to answer (because

He promises that He will), to pray fervently (because God will sometimes wait to give you an answer so that you can decide if your request is <u>really</u> what you're looking for), and to pray foremost that God's Will be done in your life and that you would not stand in its way. Remember always that as you pray, you are not bending God to your will, but you are learning to accept His will and you are forming a relationship with Him that will last throughout eternity.

CHAPTER 16:

The Purpose-Driven Prayer

Disclaimer: This chapter is not endorsed, sponsored or funded by Rick Warren, the author of The Purpose Driven Life. *It just made sense for the title and I'm pretty sure that phrase isn't copyrighted.*

I have grown up in the Christian Church and I have noticed that our prayers lack a finesse that used to typify the prayers of our forefathers.

I'm pretty sure that most of you have heard a prayer that goes something like this: "Good Lord Jesus, we just pray that You, Father, would just send your Holy Spirit, Lord God, and that He would just send help, Lord, to those that just need You, Lord God Father Jesus."

You think I'm exaggerating? I'm copying nearly word-for-word a prayer that I heard when I was younger. A friend and I made a game to count how many names of the Lord were used in this person's prayer, how many times the word "just" was used, and how many times the sub vocalization, "uh" was used (which, while being quite funny, was not very reverent).

Honestly, there are some pastors that pray like this and, as a result, a lot of us laymen do as well since we follow the examples that our pastors set for us. It seems like a lot of our prayers are riddled with space-savers. Rather than let in a thoughtful pause, we feel like we have to fill in every moment of our prayers with the names of God and the words "just," "uh," and "um."

That is depressing to me. From what I have read, the prayers of the early 20th century and further back (stretching two thousand whole years!) indicated that our fathers in the faith spoke out of the abundance of their hearts and the wisdom of their minds. And, ironically, it appears that we modern-day Christians seem to be speaking from the same places, but our wisdom and abundance are filled with empty words, meaning our minds are vacuous and our hearts are shallow.

We lack a purpose in our prayers and we no longer have the eloquence of mind to pause, compile our thoughts, and speak out in a manner that is both reasonable and intelligent. Instead of allowing for pauses in our prayers that allow us to seek the Holy Spirit and pray as we ought, we think that we can find the Holy Spirit's purpose in a multitude of words and grunts.

I suppose that the lack of eloquence is supposed to show that our prayers are unplanned and spontaneous, truly sincere, but they come across as childish and boorish.

Why is it important to pray with purpose when we are praying aloud? When we pray in our hearts, God hears us so why should we put extra effort when we pray out loud? I don't think it is so that we can appear wise or brilliant before others, but so that our prayers can edify others and bring to mind things that they had not thought of.

When we pray the "silly prayer," as I'll call it, we tend to call to mind the first thing we think of and we do not take time to think about what needs to be said. There is much to be said for not sounding like a fool before God. He already knows we are foolish; must we drive the point home by acting the part?

I'm sorry, that may have been a bit harsh, but I hope you understand that I am not just being mean for the fun of it. One can derive very little pleasure from being mean to people that they will never meet. Please remember that the way we talk to God affects those around us. If the younger Christians (I am not referring to physical age) around us hear us speaking long, rambling, silly prayers, then they will think that this is the appropriate way for them to pray and they will begin to think that it is the only way to interact with God. As such, they, too will learn to imitate our way of thinking, remembering that, if our prayers do not sound intelligent, it is possible that God does not want intelligent, reasoning, thinking followers, and as such, it becomes en vogue to check one's mind at the door.

I do not think this is God's intention for our prayers at all. I think our prayers need to follow the guideline that Jesus laid out for us in the Lord's Prayer.

Jesus begins His prayer by saying "Our Father in Heaven, hallowed be Your name." I don't think this is said to get God's attention. God does not perk up when He hears His name mentioned. I'm pretty sure He knows when His children are talking to Him, whether they actually address Him by name or not.

Rather, I think Jesus includes this introduction so that we may remember to whom we are speaking. We are speaking to our Father (more appropriately translated, "Daddy"), who loves us enough to listen to us. He lives in Heaven, so He is removed from us, but not distant from us. And His name is hallowed, or "sacred." Everything in this prayer exudes familiarity, but respect. It also brings back the awe and respect that Isaiah had for God when he called himself a man of unclean lips from a people of unclean lips. It brings to our mind the wisdom of King Solomon when, at the end of his life, he wrote, "Do not be rash with your mouth, and let not your heart utter anything hastily before God. For God is in heaven, and you on earth; therefore let your words be few. For...a fool is known by his many words."

This is why the silly prayer is bad. It does not give God respect. It fills God's ear with a lot of extra words that do not mean anything and it rambles around until it hits the point. God, who knows our request before we ask it, does not need us to wear Him out with rambling words, repetitions of His Name (in all of its various forms), or the ever-present "uhs" and "ums." He just wants us to form a simple, honest request. He wants us to feel free to be familiar with

Him, but remember that He is holy, His name is sacred, and is not something to be tossed around willy-nilly.

The outline Jesus gave us in the Lord's prayer seems to be a good example for us to follow: first He opens with an acknowledgement of who God is (Father in Heaven), He makes request for God to come quickly, hallow His name among the unbelieving World, establish His kingdom and bring earth in subjugation to His will (Your kingdom come, Your will be done on earth as it is in heaven). Jesus then moves on to petitioning God. In the Lord's Prayer, Jesus asks specifically for daily needs (bread) and for forgiveness of sin. Jesus then pleads that God keep us from temptation from the enemy, and finally moves on to praise God at the end.

Our prayers should reflect the model of praising God for who He is (our Father), requesting that He return quickly, make our requests with a contrite heart, but without fear of asking. Our prayers should request forgiveness for sins, not because our sins will not be forgiven otherwise, for God has promised that Christ's sacrifice erased all past, present, and future sins from His mind, but because when we ask for forgiveness of our sins, we remember the wrong we did and we are forced to remember that, even while saved, we are still imperfect and should not think more highly of ourselves than we ought. In the same token, we should ask to be kept from sin; to be protected and that God would guard our hearts and minds in Christ Jesus. Finally, we should always end our prayers by praising God. It doesn't matter if He gives us our request; what matters is that we, through prayer, remember who we are, who He is, and then praise Him for who He is.

Prayer is an awesome weapon in the Christian's arsenal. It is our chance to become acquainted with God, to know His will, and to learn how to accept it. Always remember; prayer is our way of talking to the all-powerful Creator of the Universe. He may not blast us into a million pieces for not knowing what we're talking about, but let's at least try to sound a little more intelligent.

CHAPTER 17

Awe and Wonder

Have you ever looked out at a grand mountain and marveled at its snow-dusted peak? Have you seen a sea of grain when the wind is blowing softly through and thought about how peaceful the rustling noises are? Have you seen a sunrise in the desert, or watched the sunset on the West Coast, when there is a mild cloud cover and stood, with mouth agape, as you take in the vast panorama of colors? If you have, then you have experienced the joy of not living in a big city and have found yourself in awe at the beauty of creation.

If you do live in a big city, then you can still see beauty amidst the chaos. You can see the sun set against the skyline. You can hear the bustle of life and ponder the modern miracle of having 5 million plus people in a single city. You can be saved by super heroes, since they always tend to gravitate towards the big cities and shy away from the countryside.

Awe is a response to something that is grand and magnificent and it produces stunned silence as man stands in wonder at something that shows the true artistic beauty of the Creator. It is hard to describe "awe" to someone that declares that they have never felt it. Personally, I do not know if it is possible for a person to look up at the stars and not realize how truly insignificant that person is and – for the Christian – to feel just how fantastic it is that God loves us anyway.

Awe is a proper response to a worthy object. It is paying respect to something that deserves to be gazed at and seems to be a subconscious salute to the Creator of the beauty and the Architect of the marvels of the universe.

However, we are not always struck by the awesome things around us, especially if we live around them all the time. As Tommy Lee Jones observed in *Men in Black,* very few people take the time to look at the stars and admire the twinkling lights. People become acclimated to these things and consider them commonplace. It is only when we allow ourselves to be receptive and look at the world through the innocent eyes of a child that we see the world for what it really is: beautiful.

I used to live in Oregon; I was surrounded by beautiful green hills and could - on the rare cloudless day - see ice-peaked mountains on the horizon. I saw these wonders of nature every day, but it was very easy to forget just how magnificent the artwork of nature really is.

In the same way, many Christians have lost their awe of God. The faith of our fathers had no room for a Christianity that did not view God as an awesome Being, worthy of fear and respect. Solomon declared that the fear of God was the beginning of wisdom, which may explain why many of us are unwise.

Many of us have the mistaken impression that God is a big, cuddly teddy bear that wouldn't harm a flea. We warm ourselves in passages like "God is love," and "All things work together for good for those who love God and are called according to His purpose."

We deliberately force ourselves to forget that God is a wrathful, jealous God that will not harbor abuse towards his chosen people, Israel, and that Jesus is very protective of His Bride, the Church (that's us). We have forgotten that God has ordered the destruction of many of the most sinful nations in the world, that He has humbled the most powerful men in the world, and that He has elevated the most humble and paltry men to positions of power. We forget that He has leveled entire cities, destroyed whole armies, has crumbled empires in a single night, and will one day bring a series of plagues on the earth that will be so terrible that nothing will have ever been like it in the history of humanity.

We choose to forget that nothing is more terrifying than to be in the hands of a just God. We choose to forget that when we think of Him, it is only fitting that we stand, eyes bulging, mouth agape, in awe of the beauty, justice, and love of God.

What does it mean to stand in awe of God? It means to provide Him the respect, fear, and admiration that He deserves. Perhaps the most awe-inspiring feature of Deity is not that He is loving or that He is powerful or that He is kind, but that He is holy. Average humans can experience love, can wield power, and can exhibit kindness; these are emotions and experiences and expressions that everybody has touched at some point or other, but holiness is a truly divine quality. It denotes purity; a complete lack of sin. Perfectly pure in every way. It means that something is whole; without blemish or stain. Though humans can be mystified by the depths to which God loves us or have our minds boggled by how powerful He is, it is the idea that He lacks some of our most defining elements, sin and imperfection, that brings us to our knees as we sing "Holy, holy, holy, Lord God Almighty, who was and is and is to come!"

We may tremble in terror before a powerful God, and it is right that we should, but it is more right that a man should quake in fear before a holy God; One in whom no there is no defect, no flaw, no imperfection of any kind. When we see the perfection of God, it is right and good that we should look at our own uncleanliness and say, as Isaiah did, "I am a man of unclean lips; I am unworthy to stand before you."

What is perhaps even more surprising is that God allows us to stand before Him and to come with boldness before Him when we are in prayer. In the ancient world, a king, Caesar, or emperor would not allow the average man to walk into his audience chamber whenever the man felt like it. Even the children of the emperors and Caesars had to exhibit restraint and decorum before their father and be very careful, lest they anger him and lose their inheritance or their lives. However, our Father not only allows us into His throne room, but encourages it and requests that we spend time in His presence so that we might learn who He is and become more familiar with Him with whom we will spend eternity.

Therefore, when you're looking at lofty mountain grandeur or hear the wind blow gently through the trees, I would encourage you to stop for a minute and put aside the anxieties that you have been feeling and allow the beauty, the wonder, the awe of the environment you are in to sweep you up. Then I would encourage you to remember the God that created these things and realize that He is even more deserving of awe and respect than these babbling brooks, or majestic animals, or beautiful landscapes.

How great, indeed, Thou art.

CHAPTER 18:

The Devil and Deception

"The greatest trick the Devil ever pulled was in convincing Man that he did not exist." Sound familiar? If you haven't read it in the introductory quotes in C.S. Lewis' *The Screwtape Letters*, then you probably heard the quote from the movie *The Usual Suspects*.

Often called the Father of Lies, the Devil (Satan, Lucifer, the Snake of Old, the Dragon, the Prince of Darkness…take your pick) really, really likes to lie to people. In fact, his sole raison d'être is to lie to the unbeliever, convincing him that God, the Devil, and the soul do not exist and, in fact, nothing exists that is not physically present in this world, or any one of a host of other lies that will keep the nonbeliever from finding the grace of Christ.

The Devil will also lie to the Christian, telling him that such-and-such a doctrine is acceptable and right when, in fact, the issue at hand is a subtle mistruth designed to offer a person a skewed perception of who God is, or that God would have them do something that is against His will, or any one of a host of other lies that will render a Christian useless and ineffective in their witness to the world.

We all know how the Devil likes to influence the nonbeliever as we see it everyday on the news or on our favorite television shows, but I find his tactics against the believer to be more relevant to me, personally.

Christians and Jews have always been a target for the Devil.

He does not have to worry too much about pagans because, frankly, they're already his (until they become saved. In which case they become God's and the Devil takes more notice of them). However, he does wage war with gusto against Christians and Jews.

Jesus warned that there would be people that would try to deceive us, either through deliberate deception, or people who would try to convert us to something that they themselves had been deceived to believe. When talking about such men, Paul said that they spread "the doctrine of demons," which implies that the preachers of lies have themselves been lied to. The sad part is, the men and women who are spreading these lies very well could have been honest, good folk who bought into a lie and, as Jesus prophesied, even the elect (Christians) were led astray.

Heresies and stuff

A heresy is any belief that tries to compromise the basics or that tries to alter the attributes of God. When a heresy becomes a system of beliefs, then that heresy has grown into a cult. Throughout history, most cults have said things like "Jesus [or the Holy Spirit] is not God." Modern cults say the same things. In fact, many big religions that claim to be "Christian" hold these age-old heretical doctrines, claiming them to be new revelations which, in fact, are just a new spin on an old idea.

Almost every blatant cult and heresy seems to tend towards letting you think that you can be "like God." Sound familiar? It should, because that was the exact error that caused Eve to stumble. The Devil, in the form of a snake, told her that she could become like God – knowing Good from Evil – if she would eat of the tree that God told her to stay away from. According to Pastor Jon Coursen, the Devil's strategy then is the same he uses today. To let you think that God is withholding something from you. To make you think that God is a cosmic bully who wants you to be repressed so that He might subjugate you to His every whim.

And, to be honest, it's entirely possible that the Devil does believe that God is baiting us for a trap. As we read in C.S. Lewis' *The Screwtape Letters*, the demons do not understand God's interest in humanity because they are incapable of love and are not able to comprehend it. Since Satan no longer trusts God and no longer serves Him, it is possible that, in his paranoia, He thinks God really is a cosmic bully. Since I've never talked directly with the Prince of Darkness, I cannot say this with any authority; I am just speculating.

No Longer off-track

Anyway, back to us being deceived.

Human curiosity always wants to know the unknown and the human condition being what it now is, if you tell us we cannot do something (and don't tell us why), we assume that you are trying to keep us from doing something that is totally awesome. That's why we violate God's law to not have sex outside of marriage. Because He doesn't give us a reason why (other than the fact that He told us not to), we automatically assume that He is a cosmic killjoy and ignore what He has to say.

Satan could not be happier than when we buy these lies!

His strategy is in three "prongs," and what was used with Eve has been used in every temptation of every man throughout history. "You shall not die. Your eyes will be opened. You will be a god." Apostle John names these three temptations as "all that is in the world," or rather, "all that the world can offer you," and labels each temptation "the lust of the flesh, the lust of the eyes, and the pride of life (1 John 2:16)."

Eve was deceived by the Devil. She looked at the tree and saw that its fruit was good for food (The lust of the flesh), she looked at the fruit and found that it was pleasant to the eyes (the lust of the eyes), and she saw that the tree was desirable to make one wise (the pride of life). And so she ate. And so humanity fell. However, we see hope against the wiles of the Devil in Jesus' life.

After He had been baptized, Jesus was led by the Holy Spirit into the desert to be tempted. The Devil came to Jesus after He had fasted for forty days and nights and He was starving. Satan tried the exact same tricks on our Lord, because the Devil's playbook is limited to three plays that tend to catch the defense off-guard.

The Devil whispered to Jesus that He should turn the rocks around Him into bread (the lust of the flesh). Jesus refused to comply, quoting that "Man shall not live by bread alone but by every word that proceeds from the mouth of God." Then the Devil took Jesus to the roof of the temple and told Him to jump off and shock the world as the angels would save Jesus from being hurt (the pride of life). Jesus was not willing to acquiesce. Finally, the Devil took Jesus to a high mountain and showed Him the kingdoms of the world and offered Him the ultimate shortcut: "Forget the cross, I'll GIVE You all the people You wanted…if You will simply worship me (the lust of the eyes)." Jesus did not suffer the Devil's presence any longer and told him to flee from Him.

So you see, the Devil has kept the same tactics for millennia and when he tried to use the same tactics on God Incarnate, the Devil failed miserably. Jesus provides us with a fantastic example: we do not have to succumb to temptation. We can look at temptation and use the Bible to combat the temptations that are assaulting us.

Are you plagued by anger? Then remember Ephesians 4:31-32: "Let all bitterness, wrath, anger, clamor and evil speaking be put away from you, with all malice. And be kind to one another, tenderhearted, forgiving one another, even as God in Christ forgave you." The Lord has promised that every temptation that assaults you is not unique to you, but is common to mankind, and that He will provide a way out of temptation so that you can endure.

When it comes to deceptions, the Devil uses the "you can become like God" trick to found entire religions. The Hindus believe in reincarnation with the goal of becoming a god and, eventually, of becoming one with the infinite universe. The Buddhists believe that one must look inward for one's eyes to be opened. The Mormons believe that, if you're a good enough Mormon, you will become a god. All these are attempts for the mortal to achieve divinity (or oblivion) through personal effort, which is the same lie the Devil has been using for millennia.

These are the religions; let's look at the anti-religion. By very definition, the atheist does not believe in God and most believe that the soul ceases to exist after death. Therefore, the Devil misleads the atheist in the exact same three ways. The atheist does not believe that he will die a second time (Hell). Since the atheist cannot pursue spirituality (because, for him, there is no spirit), he must pursue knowledge, science, philosophy, etc. His eyes are opened to the vast realm of human accomplishments and understanding once he sheds the burden that is caused by Christianity. Finally, the atheist makes himself a god (in his own mind), for he can worship nothing else but his own self, and I believe that all men must worship something; it is a basic human drive to do so.

Therefore, the Devil's tactics and strategies have remained consistent over the aeons. One would think that humanity would have caught on to his ploys, but, as was noted earlier, the Devil has convinced mankind that he does not exist, so why should anyone catch on to a plot when one does not think that there is a plotter? A diabolical mastermind, pulling strings we cannot even see?

In simple terms, the Devil's plans have generally succeeded because humans like the lies. We like the feeling of power and hidden knowledge. Therefore, it is these promises of power and knowledge that we must be wary of. Especially when the lie is carefully wrapped in truth.

The anatomy of a lie

You see, for any lie to succeed, there has to be some degree of truth to make the lie seem plausible; the greater the amount of truth content, the more likely it is that the entire lie will be palatable. Every false religion in the world has <u>some</u> element of truth to appeal to human rationality. Even worse, though, are the lies that we Christians are confronted with on a daily basis, sometimes in our own churches.

This chapter is not a witch hunt, so I will not get into any debates about whether such-and-such a doctrine is accurate. I don't care whether you are a Calvinist or Arminianist. It does not bother me if you are charismatic or evangelical. For the purposes of this book, it does not matter if you are a strict Catholic or a loose Protestant. Although there are <u>definite</u> differences between each of these three distinctions, they are so big that entire books can (and have) been written about them. I am not nearly so ambitious as to offer my opinions about each. The differences between these probably require a more expert opinion, which I do not have.

Therefore, I will have to limit myself to pointing out how to recognize some of the subtler lies that have crept into the Church. As mentioned earlier, every lie must be encased in some truth. It is like wrapping a little ball of poop in a larger ball of fudge. At first you think "Woohoo, fudge!" but inside, unbeknownst to you, is the nasty, disease-ridden poo.

The best way to identify these little lies is to keep your Bible handy. If you go to a church that does not preach out of the Bible but out of some book that is popular among Christians, then I would encourage you to seek the greener pastures of a more Bible-based church. The Bible is authoritative, given by God, and is useful for doctrine, correction, rebuking (in love), and for instruction in righteousness that every man and woman of God may be a complete individual, ready to do any good work that God may call him to do. Without the Bible, a man might as well fall asleep at the wheel of his car, assuming that "cruise control" is the same thing as "auto-pilot."

How do people, good Christians, come to support and invent lies? Well, I believe that Paul gave the answer to fledgling pastor, Timothy. Paul said that "the purpose of the commandment is love from a pure heart, from a good conscience, and from sincere faith, from which some, having strayed, have turned aside to idle talk, desiring to be teachers of the law, understanding neither what they say nor the things which they affirm. (1st Timothy, 1:5-7, NKJV)"

In other words, some supporters of these dangerous teachings do so because they have lost the simplicity of the gospel and have added requirements for our salvation, or, as in other cases, have made the gospel so simplistic that "little things" like sin and redemption are removed from the equation. In the name of "love," these pastors have ceased to truly love their congregations as the pastors are holding peoples' hands on the way to Hell, whispering to them that there is no such thing as sin and no eternal punishment awaiting the sinful.

Then they infuse the Church with little ideas that are not necessarily heretical, but that are unbiblical and lead people astray. For instance, claiming territory for Christ. The concept behind this term, as I understand it, is that a person or group of persons will pray (often loudly) that a certain city be released from the Devil's hold and that the people in it be claimed by God. Look through the Bible. The only time a person "claimed a city" was when they were going to conquer it and destroy everything within it. Are these modern-day Christians proposing that they will "conquer a city for Christ?" What is it that we are supposed to kill within these cities? That sounds vaguely like the philosophy of the Medieval Crusaders. God forbid we try to relive that debacle.

The point is, the apostles did not do this and, as a rule, if someone is preaching a new idea that is not mentioned in the Bible, then the odds are that it is a very, very poor idea to go along with what the man is telling you to do. Whenever you are presented with something "new," you should search your Bible.

When Paul went to the city of Berea, he preached Christ to those that lived in the city, and more specifically, to the Jews. These Jews accepted Paul's words gladly, BUT they daily poured over the scriptures – specifically the prophecies in the Old Testament – to see if Jesus really could be the Messiah they were looking for.

Take note of the Bereans. They were told something new. It sounded very good to them. They wanted to believe. But before they would allow themselves to believe, they had to make sure that what they were told passed the test of Scripture.

Whenever someone tells you about some new blessing from Toronto, or tells you to evangelize and "reach out" to your community by showing the "fun side" of Christianity, check to see if what is offered is endorsed by Jesus, is mentioned in the Scriptures, and is practiced by the apostles. Otherwise, you run the risk of preaching a Gospel that does not really exist. For example, "come to Christianity if you are sad and lonely because Jesus will fill you up and you'll never feel sad again."

This is true, that God is the Father to the fatherless, but this is not how we should be reaching to people. If you're going to tell them the good news, then tell them some GOOD NEWS. Any religion, practiced with earnest, can fill a person with a sense of self-satisfaction and any 12-step program can reform a person from a type of action. We have to get to the heart of the matter.

The Good News of Jesus Christ

You and I are sinners. You and I have rebelled against God. Rather than let us blindly continue in our rebellion, God loved us so much that He became a human, lived thirty-three years among us so that He could relate to us and show us that He was approachable, and then, when He had proven to us that we could not save ourselves, He took on all the sin of the entire world and died in our place. To show that He had power over life and death and to show us that death would have no power over us, He rose from the dead three days after He had lain in a tomb. Now you can be forgiven of your sins, if you choose to be. Now you can be close to God, if you choose to be. Now you can have peace, if you choose it.

This is the Good News – the Gospel – of Jesus Christ. It involves acknowledging that we sinners are separate from God, that God loves us and became a Man to show us how we can come near to God - as a man comes near to his friend, and then died for us so that we could be close to God and forgiven of sins. The penalty of not receiving this message? Hell. All actions have consequences, and the consequence of not choosing God is to choose to be separate from God.

That is what we should be preaching to people because if we are not preaching a true Gospel that preaches forgiveness from sins and a reconciliation with God, then we are holding people's hands as they go into Hell.

Does the idea of telling a person that they are a sinner sound offensive to you? Good. Jesus said that it would be. He said that the Gospel He offered would tear apart best friends and families. But the truth is worth it. The reward is worth it. Knowing that you are a sinner and then being cleansed of your sin is a feeling like none other. And knowing God…is indescribable. How can a person know God if their sins are not forgiven? And how can their sins be forgiven if we do not tell them that they are sinners? And how can we tell the world of its sin if we are not first cleansed of the sin within us? They are all questions worth asking yourself and worth wondering if you are living your Christianity in the way that God would want you to.

If you and I are going to live as Christians in this world, we have to be wary of the deceptions of the Devil, telling us to follow our own dreams apart from God, tempting us to be like Him, and tempting us to water down the Good News of Jesus by either adding to or subtracting from the full message. Avoid deception; be wary if you think you stand firm, because the Devil uses pride to deceive us.

CHAPTER 19:

Evolution, and Other Red Herrings

Just about every Christian knows the biblical account of Creation. The Bible says that in six days, God spoke into existence the cosmos and all that is within them and on the seventh day He rested as a sign to mankind that they should do the same every seventh day of the week.

The biblical account of Creation was largely uncontested from around 400 A.D. – 1800 A.D. Of course, you had oddballs like Voltaire saying that God did not exist, or random offshoots of Christianity (read: cults), like Mormonism and the Jehovah's Witnesses. However, it wasn't until Charles Darwin published his book, *The Origin of Species* that the biblical account of a six-day creation came into serious question.

For a long while, most Christians ignored evolution, finding it offensive that anyone would claim that Man came from a monkey. The "goo to the zoo to you" philosophy that was spouted by evolutionists was considered laughable by most of the public, although many intellectuals had picked up on it. Of course, this isn't because those in academia are so much smarter than the rest of us, it's just that they had been looking for an excuse to not believe in God, and evolution provided the intellectual excuse that the intelligentsia were looking for.

It wasn't until the Scopes Monkey Trial in the 1930s that Christianity had to come face-to-face with the widespread nature of evolution and realize that it (Christianity) was unprepared to defend itself. To give you the Cliff's Notes version, the Scopes Monkey Trial was a lawsuit against a school teacher who was illegally teaching evolution to his students. During the trial, the defense attorney decided that, rather than defend his client, he was going to make a precedent-setting case by tearing apart the difficult questions in the Bible. Therefore, the defense interrogated the prosecutor about where Cain found his wife, and other questions that the Bible does not provide a simple answer for. The prosecutor did not have an answer for the tough questions – not because there are no answers, but because he had never thought about them.

The jury wound up convicting the teacher, but it set a bad precedent for Christians and gave us a bad name as pseudo-intellectual wackos.

Let's fast forward about 70 years. In my college days, I saw Christians respond three different ways to evolution: they either hate it, thinking it is the root of all evil, they support it, believing that God used evolution to create the cosmos, or they don't really care one way or the other.

Well, I don't really want to address the second perspective because, in all honesty, I don't know whether or not God used evolution. I'm pretty sure the Creation account is accurate to a "T," but there are elements that I have yet to understand, such as why there are only dinosaur fossils, but no cow or chicken or dog fossils. Of course, evolution has an equally insurmountable problem of having no fossils of transitional species (a platypus is not a transitional species).

What I want to cover is the attitude implied by the first and the last perspective (hate evolution or do not care). In my college years, there was always one man that would come onto the campus with a sandwich board that said "Evolution is an adult fairytale." This man would then proceed to verbally spar with people that would challenge his opinion, occasionally shouting them down, often being generally rude to the public at large. He would attack believer and nonbeliever alike. This man, though zealously opposed to evolution, had forgotten something: atheism (and similar worldviews) are not the disease that we have been sent to warn others of, but it is instead a symptom of that disease. Of course, the disease I am referring to is sin.

This man had allowed the Devil to sidetrack him with a very tempting red herring. A distraction that seems like a legitimate thing to complain against, but in reality, it distracts from the real issue of a person's need for Jesus.

We, as Christians, have been sent out to make disciples of all nations. If we are to warn them of anything, we are to warn them of the penalty of their sin, but do so out of love as we keep telling them that the disease is only fatal if left untreated. Because, you see, there is a fantastic cure to sin: Jesus. We are supposed to preach Jesus to people.

I know that I have often fallen off of this bandwagon. I have found demons lurking in every shadow. One day, it's evolution; the next day, it's abortion; the following day, it's liberalism. None of these things are the giant that we have been sent to slay, but it sure is tempting to try to bring that giant down!

What we often forget is that in waging a war against abortion (evolution, liberalism, communism, antidisestablishmentarianism, etc), we leave behind the people that we are supposed to love. We either alienate them or we flat out attack them as if they were the enemy. The Bible makes it very clear that our battle is not against people, but is rather against the demons that are propagating the deceptions that are driving the people. We fight ideas, not people. We are the only army that is not interested in killing the enemy, but is interested in taking back prisoners from the enemy. Why is this? Because Jesus already defeated Satan (the enemy) at the cross. Our job is to show nonbelievers (the "prisoners" in this little metaphor) that they are free from their captivity, and all they have to do is step out from the shadows and claim that freedom.

Guys, let's remember that we are to act out in love towards our neighbor. Sometimes we employ what we cynically call "hard love," such as when we explain about sin and Hell, but this has to be followed with a presentation of "soft love" (I dunno…making up terms here) where we talk about the "good news" part of the Gospel.

Therefore, going back to the point I was trying to make at the beginning of the chapter, I do not care much about evolution, and I do not believe that abortion is where we should focus our energies. Though these are tactics and institutions used by the devil to take both lives and souls, I think that they are "red herrings;" tactics that are used to distract from the really important issue of a man's unredeemed soul.

It is possible that the Devil uses these issues to cloud our minds, making us focus on the good and noble goal of trying to disprove a lie, but then this makes us forget that we are supposed to reveal truth to people. It seems like the kind of trick that he would use because it is using a lesser truth to distract from a greater truth. Be wary of the Devil and his schemes, he likes to use the rope-a-dope philosophy of showing one very real danger, but sneaking in a much more potent and devastating hit that sends us reeling. We need to realize that, even in our various crusades against wrong (evolution, abortion, gay marriage, lower taxes…whatever), there are people that are watching us and are judging Christianity – and, by association, are judging Christ – based on your actions and on the way you fight your war against [insert controversial topic here].

Don't let your war against the lies of the Devil bring forth collateral damage. Don't let the souls of the people you are trying to disprove become casualties. Remember the Gospel in the midst of your picket lines.

CHAPTER 20:

Throwing the First Stone

Jesus was faced with a catch-22. The Pharisees, sticklers for the Law of Moses, had found a woman caught in the act of adultery, dragged her to Jesus, and demanded that Jesus tell them what they should do with the woman. In the Pharisees' eyes, if Jesus went by the Law of Moses, then He would say that the woman should be stoned, but because the Romans did not permit the Jews to carry out death sentences without Roman approval, He would be breaking the Roman law, advocating rebellion from the established authority. However, if He were to say that they should show mercy, then they could claim that He was violating the Law of Moses by not ordering her to be executed, and He would lose credibility when He said that He had not come to destroy the Law but fulfill it.

Whichever way Jesus went, the Pharisees thought they had Him trapped.

Here's the deal, though. The Pharisees, in their zeal to disprove Jesus, forgot the very scriptures that they claimed to know so well. The Bible says that they "caught her in the act of adultery." With whom? Where is the man? You have to have two to tango, and you can't catch a woman adulterating if you don't have a man in the mix somewhere.

I have heard it speculated that the man was himself a Pharisee, which means that the Pharisees hated Jesus so much that they would violate their own Law to catch Him. Either way, Jesus did not take the bait. Instead of playing their little game, He appears to ignore them and starts doodling on the ground, allowing them time to stew in their own self-righteous juices.

The Bible doesn't record what He wrote. It could have been a record of all of their sins, it could have been an account of this particular plot against Him, including the name of the offending male, it could have been a comic strip. No one knows. We do know, however, that the Pharisees – like the whining children that they were – pestered Jesus for an answer.

When they kept demanding an answer, He replied to them: "He who is without sin among you, let him throw a stone at her first." Jesus, implying that everyone involved in this plot against Him knew that one among them had sinned and had therefore sinned themselves, is saying that they all deserve death, and if any of them are innocent of the matter, they should lob the first stone. Of course, none of them were innocent.

Either way, after Jesus issued this statement, all of the Pharisees, starting with the oldest – and supposedly "wisest" – left the scene, abandoning the woman so that she was alone with Jesus. He asked her if there stood no one left to condemn her. She replied that there was no one there. He then stated that He did not condemn her either and that she should go her way and stop sinning. Now, of course, this was neither a suggestion nor a harsh command. It was a statement that said that, though she had been forgiven of her sins, she should live uprightly. Which now leads us to the purpose of this chapter; to examine the tendency for Christians to judge other Christians. Should we or shouldn't we?

Jesus gives us a very clear example that has often been horribly misinterpreted and riddled with inaccuracies. Many people look at this event, captured in the book of John, and say, "See!?! We should not confront people with sin because we are judging and condemning them. If Jesus did not do it, neither should we!"

These people have good intentions, but, of course, the road to Hell is paved with good intentions. The followers of this belief do not see that Jesus told the woman that He did not <u>condemn</u> her, which does not mean that He was not calling her actions sinful. She knew what she did was wrong. Everyone who heard the Pharisees' accusations knew what she did and knew she had sinned against God. Jesus did not try to dispute the Pharisees by claiming that she might have been innocent. Instead, Jesus said that He would forgive her, that He would show her mercy, because she certainly was not going to get mercy from the Pharisees who tricked her.

Jesus was never one for calling a donkey a horse. When there was sin around, He let people know it, but He also forgave the repentant. Who were the repentant? Those who, when confronted with their sin, felt guilty, knew they were wretches that needed forgiveness. To these, Jesus offered forgiveness. He even pled for forgiveness for the Pharisees and the Romans who executed Him, for they did not know they were killing God Incarnate. But He never, ever claimed that a person who was sinning was not sinning. Jesus loved people too much to lie to them.

You see, for forgiveness to be present, sin has to be present first and Jesus would not forgive a person who had not sinned. Where am I going with this? Very simple. Christians need to stop calling a donkey a horse. We need to stop being afraid that a person will think that we are "judging them" when we tell them, in love, that their actions are sinful, but their sins can be forgiven. How else can a person be saved if their sinfulness is not brought before them and the way of salvation offered to them?

Herein lies an irony, however. The Church (I use a capital "C" because I think it a near universal malady that afflicts the entire Church body) is cowardly when it comes to convicting the world of their sin, but when it comes to alienating and condemning Christians for sin, the Church is eager to pounce. Like sharks drawn to blood, Christians seem drawn towards the scent of a wounded Christian. In other words, the Church will not confront one of their own in love to tell them of that Christian's sin and help lead them away from it, but once that person has fallen on hard times as a result of sin and is reaping the inevitable fruit of sin, the Church will pounce on them like a cat pounces on catnip.

It has been aptly stated that the Army of Christ is the only army in history that will shoot its own wounded.

And it is all so simple for us on how to deal with a sinning believer, for Jesus GAVE us the formula to use in Matthew chapter 18, verses 15-17. First, if someone sins against you, go to them directly and discuss it in love, man-to-man (woman-to-woman). If they do not listen, take a fellow Christian or two to help. If the sinning Christian still does not listen, tell the church, openly, to prevent gossip and to keep everything out in the open. If the sinning Christian still does not listen, then the church is to disassociate with the sinning Christian, for he has obviously decided that he will not listen to wise counsel. All this is to be done in love, of course, for the goal is to help redeem the sinner, not to push him away. The very act of telling someone that they are in the wrong is isolating enough; to take it a step further with inappropriate actions would be sin itself.

I am not so much levying this accusation at the individual Christian, because we laymen are very guilty of such sin, but the thing is, we take after the example of our leaders. And I am going to be a bit stern here, because I believe that a great disservice has been done to the Christians of America.

Pastors, I must say that I am ashamed and disgusted with many of you. You have your job description laid out, very clearly, in 1 Timothy, chapter 3. You are to be blameless, husband of one wife, temperate (not a drunk), sober-minded (not a fool), of good behavior (not known for being a troublemaker), hospitable (merciful), able to teach, not given to wine (not an alcoholic), not violent, but gentle, not quarrelsome (don't pick fights with people, either in your church or outside of it), not covetous (guys, don't want what you can't have but that someone else does have, be it a bigger church building, or more people in the pews, or more money in your coffers), one who rules his house well, having his children in submission with all reverence (if you are letting your children run rampant, then you have failed this qualification); not a novice (new believers should wait a bit before they take the plunge, but I don't think this means you have to go to seminary to be a pastor).

Moreover you must have a good testimony among those who are not Christians, otherwise, you run the risk of being scorned by the nonbelievers, not because of your witness for Christ, but because of your own hypocrisy [this was a paraphrase of the first 7 verses of 1st Timothy, chapter 3].

That last requirement – having a good testimony – is a stumbling block for many good men. In wanting everyone else to like them, these pastors have bought into a social gospel that lets people see that "hey, Christians aren't so bad," but they neglect to mention that "Oh yeah, if you're without Christ, you're going to Hell."

It has hurt me that, in many churches today, the pastor and elders will cast people out the fellowship, simply because the person want a divorce – oftentimes, these divorces are for good reason, but sometimes not.

Are we going to start justifying our sins? Because there is no justification for them. If you have gotten a divorce and remarried, then the Bible says that you have committed adultery, but you know what? There is forgiveness. Jesus has forgiven every Christian's sins, be they past, present, or future. A person should never try to justify themselves with reasons and excuses for any sin, be it adultery, divorce, homosexuality, unjust anger, etc, but rest in the fact that they have been forgiven and move on with their lives. There is such an abundance of mercy that a man or woman who has sinned and been forgiven should simply say "I sinned, I have been forgiven, and I am moving on."

And that is where I think the command "judge not, lest ye be judged" comes into play. Should we help a brother who is sinning? Yes. Should we temporarily exclude them from the Church if they continue unrepentant? Yes. But we have to be very careful that we are judging actions and not person. We can tell a person, "Jerry, you are sinning, I know you know that you are. You should stop," but we cannot tell a person, "Jerry, you are sinning and have therefore crossed the line. I cannot be around you anymore because you are an evil man."

We cannot say this because Jesus says that we will be judged by the same standard by which we judge other people – whether that be on a temporal or eternal timeframe, I'm not sure, but Jesus said that it was going to happen, so I'm fairly certain we can count on it happening.

It may seem like I am not following my own recommendations by judging pastoral conduct. I can see that. It is a very fair accusation, but it ignores some things. First of all, I am not judging based on my own standard; I am judging based on the standard that was passed down to them by God to the Apostle Paul to Pastor Timothy. And, to be honest, I am upset at the conduct that I see in many of today's pastors in being almost eager to lob stones at weak and wounded congregation members. These are the ones that were wolves hidden among the sheep whose goal it was to fleece the flock.

Pastors and laymen alike need to surround the people around us who are sinning. We should lovingly warn them to stay away from their sin. If they become hurt by their sin, we should not gloat about it, saying "I told you so," but we should comfort them; help them; love them. I'm fairly certain that it is what Jesus would do.

CHAPTER 21:

Meekness; Not a Bad Thing, After All

We Christians are branded as a lot of things, most of which are contradictory. We are considered to be both incredibly arrogant and doormats; we are warhawks, but are also called spineless cowards; we are stupid, yet still are cunning enough to ruin the nation. Part of this is based on the world's absolute bias against us, but we also have to sift through the rhetoric to see that there is some truth in these accusations. Now, one chapter in this book discusses politics and war, but this chapter is devoted to the arrogance that we Christians seem to be cursed with.

Several thousand years ago (like, around two thousand), Jesus said some pretty impressively depressing things: He said stuff like, "Blessed are the poor in spirit" in a world where feeling good about life and yourself was very popular. He said "Blessed are the peacemakers," in a society where people sued for every small grievance and warred at will. And He said "Blessed are the meek," in a land where arrogance and self-esteem were the primary virtue. Oddly enough, the Roman-Jewish world of 30 A.D. sounds very similar to the American-European-everywhere-else world that we currently live in.

Anyway, meekness is the virtue that we seem to be lacking, mainly because we seem to be lacking a good definition of what meekness really is. Because no one really understands what meekness is supposed to be, we decide that, since "meekness" rhymes with "weakness," to be meek is automatically to be weak. If people think that Christians are to be weak, and that the weak are the ones that are to be blessed, then it is perfectly legitimate for people to walk over Christians while Christians lie on the ground like dirt, waiting for the feet to land.

"Blessed are the wallflowers, for they might not get noticed, Blessed are the doormats, for they shall be walked upon, Blessed are the pathetic, for we might take pity on them."

Some pastors may preach this; I've heard it before and I'm sure there are plenty of verses a man could use to support this belief, but I take a different opinion, so I would advise you to weigh my argument against the Bible and see if it's accurate.

From the context of the Bible, meekness does not mean the ability to be weak, but to be unobtrusive; to not seek yourself out; to not lord your authority and power – assuming you have any – over others. Therefore, meekness is a trait that we would love to see in our leaders, but once we see a person that is too meek, we cannot help but loathe them. We wish they would stand up for themselves; it's like watching a movie from the 1980s about that one nerdy kid that keeps letting the bullies pick on him. You want to join in with the bullies and pound the nerd until he grows a backbone – but, of course, he never does.

Meekness is the exact opposite of arrogance because arrogance seeks to promote oneself, while meekness will not gloat or boast. For the Christian, meekness points to Christ. Christian meekness says "I'll speak about God and not about myself." We must decrease so that He might increase. We must die to self and live in the life that Christ offers.

Of course, when we accept that we are to be meek, we run the risk of swinging in the opposite direction of arrogance and become spineless Christians, unwilling or unable to stand up for anything. So, in order to provide a good example of how we are to live, let me reference a few people in the Bible that are listed as meek: Moses and Jesus.

Moses is called the meekest man in the entire nation of all Israel. At the time, Moses was the mouthpiece of God, the middleman between God and the nation of Israel. He used to be the adopted son of a princess of Egypt. If any one of us would have the right to be arrogant in their own position in life, Moses had even more right, but he did not let his position go to his head. He cared for the flock he shepherded and did not allow his own natural, human desires for lording power over others to influence how he led or how he viewed himself.

However, Moses is not the ultimate example of what meekness should be, for we see that Jesus had even more reason to be arrogant than Moses. Jesus was/is Lord of Creation. In the book of John, we see that the world was created through Jesus and that everything was created for the sole purpose of His enjoyment. When He came to earth, He had every right to come down with thunder and lightning, striking dead the Pharisees and Romans, and establish an immediate rule on earth.

Acting in typical God-like fashion, Jesus did not come in the manner we would expect, but instead was born into the family of a poor carpenter and was most likely considered a bastard-child because Mary was not married to Joseph at the time she conceived Jesus (even though the Bible assures us that she was a virgin). He became lowly and took on our sins, becoming as gentle as a lamb so that He might become our example for how we should conduct ourselves.

Of course, in every instance that Jesus stands as an example, the world tries to convince us to be something different. Where Jesus was gentle and forgiving, the world tries to convince us to make ourselves better than others and to focus on others' faults so that we might think that we are superior to those around us.

Meekness is not weakness; it is gentleness, it is humbleness, it is Christ-like. It is difficult to be meek because it runs contrary to our nature, but if the Bible tells us that we are to be meek, then you can rest assured that God will help us achieve this state of being, for, as in all things, we should not embark on improving ourselves without realizing that we must be led, directed, and aided by God if we are to have any lasting change in our lives.

Paul calls us ambassadors to Christ and that is what we are. An ambassador is a man or woman who lives in a foreign country and represents the authority of the sovereign from the ambassador's homeland. Christians are foreigners who live on earth. Our citizenship is in Heaven. Therefore, we must bear in mind that our words are direct reflections on the King we represent. As such, it is vitally necessary that we keep an eye on what we say and how we represent ourselves.

We are taught in elementary school that it does not matter what others think of us, but this is only a half-truth. No Christian should ever pander to the whims of society or pop culture. Instead, we should care what people think of us because they will make a direct correlation between our actions and the actions of God. If Christians act arrogant and unloving, then the world thinks that God is the same way. If Christians treat other Christians with contempt, then the world thinks that we are a country divided, in the midst of a civil war and on the brink of collapse. However, if we act with love towards one another then the world will see God for who He really is. That is not to say that the world will love us. Nope, Jesus said it wouldn't. We can, at least, be good ambassadors, speaking as ones that have direct contact with God, for we really do, in the words of the Bible, in the speaking of the Spirit, and in the solitude of prayer.

Christian meekness is not weak, for no one would say that Christ was weak. He was so emotionally stable that people were shocked the few times he cried, and He was not stern and grumpy, because children loved to run up to Him. Christian meekness is a reserved strength that says "I may be an ambassador and I may carry all the authority and power that come with the title, but I am a servant as well, and I shall not let my role as ambassador interfere with my role as servant."

Be a royal ambassador. Be meek, and show what Christ was like to a world that does not understand Him.

CHAPTER 22:

Tolerance

Tolerance is a peculiar word. Nowadays, it has become a character trait that is more important than personal virtue.

The modern definition of tolerance implies that we should look at every lifestyle and choice as a good, natural decision. It goes beyond accepting the decision into accepting the person <u>for</u> their decision.

I'll just point out the elephant in the room: the main thing that Christians are expected to be tolerant of is homosexuality. Everyone around us expects us to look at homosexuality and applaud the fact that they feel free to do it with whomever they like. Of course, the world knows that we will not accord to this definition of tolerance because the many evangelical Christians in the world look at their Bibles and see that a man should not approve of things that the Bible expressly calls sinful.

Therefore, if anything, Christians are called to a more ancient (read: 1950s and earlier) definition of the word "tolerance." This definition states that "I have judged such and such and have decided that I cannot approve of it, but I can decide to live at peace with those that choose to live their lives in a way that I view to be morally wrong."

Of course, the world cannot abide this definition of tolerance because the world demands approval, and so we are constantly at odds.

But the just God who rules the universe is uncompromising. He does not ignore sin or pretend it does not exist. The very nature of God cannot accept that which is rebellion and direct disobedience to who He is, so whenever the world says we are to call black, "white," we <u>must</u> look at black and call it "black."

What the world wants from us, we cannot and should not give. Where we are expected to compromise, we must stand resolute. Where we are expected to cave, we must never give up or give in.

Tolerance is a virtue because it allows people to live in harmony that share contradictory beliefs. Tolerance was a virtue that the Romans prided themselves on because, though they may have disagreed with the religious beliefs of an area that they had conquered, as long as those religions did not violate Roman law, the Romans were content to let the people keep their religion. It was only when the Jews and the Christians refused to bow before Caesar as god that the Romans became especially intolerant. Obviously, the Romans are not a perfect example of how people should be tolerant as they tended to crucify any person, city, or nation that would step outside of their boundaries. Unfortunately, however, we have to look at a pagan empire to see a good example of what tolerance should be like, for there has never been another empire - Christian or otherwise - that has allowed so much freedom to so many people, even in America.

American "Tolerance"

Americans like to pride themselves on being enlightened and tolerant beings, but we have a bloody history that is rife with hating Catholics, Indians, Mormons, etc. We drove the Mormons out of Missouri and Illinois, forcing them to move West. We killed thousands of Indians, sometimes justified, oftentimes not. We had a general distrust and dislike for Catholics in our early days because the Founding Fathers - those who were Christians - were part of the

Church of England, which specifically broke off from the Roman Catholic Church centuries ago.

Then, of course, we have the slavery issue, the Japanese interment camps, etc, etc, etc. Nowadays, America is largely intolerant of biblical Christianity, a viewpoint that is mocked in the media, by celebrities, and by the intelligentsia.

Aren't we just so advanced? Look at how tolerant we are of those that differ from us!

Tolerance is the virtue of seeing an opposing viewpoint and accepting it, not necessarily as valid, but accepting the person's right to have that viewpoint. However, not every viewpoint can be tolerated. Some must be corrected and as Christians, it is our duty to go out into the world and tell people the Good News of Jesus and thereby show them grace, tolerance, and mercy.

It seems silly to repeat something I have said in another chapter, but we Christians forget this concept frequently: when we go to correct someone or to witness to another person, we cannot pretend that we are better than that person or don a haughty attitude. We must come to the people we are witnessing to as Christ did; in all humility. We must humble ourselves to the position of servants, because, as Christians, we are servants of Christ and therefore can be used to serve other people.

Tolerance can be described in three different words: grace, mercy, and charity. Grace is giving someone something they don't deserve; mercy is <u>not</u> giving someone the punishment they deserve, and charity is giving yourself to someone who may or may not deserve such devotion.

The Other Shoe

However, guys, realize that just because you tolerate other people does not mean that other people will tolerate you. In fact, they will do the exact opposite.

The world insists that it is very tolerant, but as soon as a person or religion crosses their line and declares that such-and-such is wrong, the world clamps its iron jaws and refuses to tolerate that person or religion any more. In this way, Christianity is a very intolerant religion. It declares an objective standard of morality and states that any deviations from this standard are wrong.

The world does not like this, so it has invented the wonderfully contradictory view called "postmodernism." Postmodernism is ridiculous to the point of being hilarious – or, at least, it is in theory. Postmodernism is a very complex worldview because it states that a person's worldview may change at the drop of a hat and that their morality is largely dependant on whatever they want it to be at any given point and time. Confused? Good. That's just what the postmodernist wants. Don't get me wrong, postmodernists are just as confused as we are about the whole concept, but they don't want you to know that because the gaps in their worldview are so broad that two trucks could, in tandem, drive through their arguments.

I was a part of a club that sponsored debates between Christians and non-Christians and pitted them in the arena of science, modern culture, etc. As often as we could, the Socratic Club – for that's what it was called – would bring in experts from both sides of the argument so that both sides could be represented with a degree of equality. We never wanted one side to complain that we had been setting them up to take a fall.

In my time at the Socratic Club, I saw many postmodernist thinkers. Since the members of the Socratic Club often had to endure lectures from professors that stated that there were absolutely no moral absolutes – a belief that is very common in postmodernism – we were interested to see how a postmodernist would defend their beliefs. Almost every time, the postmodernist would wiggle his or her way away from any pointed question that would force the postmodernist to admit to what they actually believed. I am personally of the opinion that this was because the postmodernist had no clue what they believed.

Postmodernism is the ultimate in worldly tolerance because it allows everyone to have their own opinion, as long as they do not tread on the postmodernist's toes. Then all Hell breaks loose.

The world can tolerate anything but the intolerance of the Cross, and that is how it should be. Jesus said it would happen, and lo and behold, it happens. We constantly hear of people from the ACLU tearing down this institution, or some member of the Supreme Court ruling against this Christian ideal. It's the world we live in and it is not going to get better until Jesus comes back.

So, what this means is that even though everyone hates us, we still must tolerate them. Love them despite their hatred towards us. Show grace, mercy, and charity to those that would persecute you; pray for your enemies. It may be difficult at times and we may find someday that we Christians will live in constant peril because of our "intolerance," but that is what Jesus promised. Remember, the world hated Him, so it's going to hate us, too.

CHAPTER 23:

Pain, Death, and Grief

Death and the fear of death have struck ever single one of us. Not always is death physical, but it can be vocational ("Steve, we're going to have to let you go."), relational ("I just don't love you anymore"), or physical ("Sir, I have some bad news; it's a malignant tumor, lodged in your brain. We cannot operate."), or fictional ("He's dead, Jim").

We have all felt the icy grip of fear come over us as we dread losing the job, breaking off the relationship, or dying. Therefore, it seems absolutely insane to say "Brethren, rejoice in tribulation," but the Bible is insistent: we must be glad when we are in pain.

Rejoicing when you are hurting most is contrary to human nature. We want to be happy only when life is going our way. If possible, we want to avoid every pratfall or divot in the road that we can. When life goes wrong, we'd rather curl up and die than face whatever it is we are having to deal with. But God did not give us that option. In fact, Jesus said that "in this world, you will have trouble. But fear not, for I have overcome the world." I want you to look over that sentence (well, two sentences) again. What stands out? If you answered anything other than "fear not," than look again.

Everywhere, *everywhere* Jesus, God, angels, and apostles are telling us not to fear. I propose two reasons for this: 1) It is in human nature to fear the unknown. 2) We shouldn't.

Christians have no need to fear the unknown, death, pain, etc. Paul gives us our reason: Tribulations build character, character builds perseverance, perseverance builds hope and hope does not disappoint. Let's break that into its constituent parts.

Tribulation: easy word, means…something in Greek. Probably something really, really bad. Let's assume, for the sake of accuracy, that it means "pressing," as in the pressing of olives to get at the oil that lurks inside. A "tribulation" with relations to the human equation is a figurative pressing (crushing, if you will) of a person. Tribulations can come in the form of persecution (if you've been a Christian for 10 years and have never been persecuted, you're probably doing something wrong [see Matthew 5:10-12]), it can come in the form of the fear of death (remember, socially, financially, physically), it can be that constant twinge of pain in your back that reminds you that your body is rapidly aging, or tribulation can take the form of death itself (of a dog, coworker, friend, loved one, or yourself). Each of these events are painful and devastating, but Paul says we are supposed to rejoice.

How? How can the New Testament authors claim that we, in our weakest, most vulnerable moments, are supposed to be glad that we are being ripped apart by the pains of life, the hatred of our fellow man, or torn asunder by the loathing of demonic forces?

I suggest we look to Jesus (the author and perfecter of our faith), who, for the joy set before Him, overcame the cross, scorning its shame, and sat down at the right hand of God [see Hebrews 12]. Jesus was known as the man of sorrows. Why was He the "man of sorrows?" Sounds like a film noir title, doesn't it? Jesus was the man of sorrows because He knew the past, present, and future from an eternal perspective, but still saw all of us humans running around with our temporal perspectives. How, then, if He is surrounded by a bunch of blind sheep who were constantly running off cliffs or running into each other, be said to have endured the cross joyfully?

Especially when you consider what the cross was. Mel Gibson had the right idea, I think, but he left out one critical detail: the cross that Christ endured was not horrific for the physical torture. For

Jesus, that pain ended in 12 hours, and there are some people that are tortured for weeks upon months who have suffered more physical pain than Jesus did. I would respectfully submit that the man in the concentration camp or the lady dying of cancer, or the Protestant on the rack knows more about physical pain than Jesus did.

No, the horror of the cross came when Jesus accepted the guilt and the penalty for EVERY sin that mankind ever had committed and was ever going to commit. That is a burden that it is impossible for us to even imagine.

Think of it this way. Let us assume that you are eight-years-old. You are a little hellion, causing trouble and property damage wherever you can. One day, you are playing a game of baseball. You step up to the plate (which is a literal dinner plate); you take a few practice swings with your bat; the pitcher winds up as only little boys can; you swing wildly at the ball and *SMACK* you connect! The ball sails higher, higher, slightly less high, much less high, lower, until *CRASH* you have broken Mr. Macready's dining room window.

Well, as with all people that do something bad, your first reaction is "Crap! I'm going to be in trouble!!" so you run home. Eventually, your friends rat you out to their parents and their parents call your parents. Your parents are quite displeased with you. Being the verbose people that they are, your parents sit you down and proceed to rake you over the coals for breaking a window, and then lying about it. If you are any kind of decent human being, you feel very guilty, which is the point of the lecture. Your parents wanted to make sure you knew what was right and what was wrong.

Now that you are remembering the guilt you felt, let's crank that up a bit. Imagine all of the broken windows in the world, and feeling the collective guilt for that. Hard to imagine, isn't it? Now take that a step further and feel all the guilt for all of the sinful acts ever committed with a baseball bat. That gets even harder, doesn't it? Now, imagine every sin and every wrongdoing ever committed, whether it is a white lie or a heinous triple homicide, or the guilt of murdering an entire village. Here we get into the realm of the impossible as we cannot comprehend every sin ever committed.

So how was Jesus' experience on the cross joyful? How did He find joy in the most miserable situation that could ever afflict a person? Simple. He kept perspective. He knew that better was awaiting Him. He was going to be crowned the King of Kings, Lord of Lords. He was going to sit before His Father as the final High Priest that mankind would ever need, as His one sacrifice would forever cleanse us of our sins. He was going to enjoy fellowship with His Father, but He would also enjoy fellowship with us.

In the garden of Gethsemane, Jesus placed Himself in accordance with the Father's will when He said those words that should forever be on the lips of every Christian, "Not My will, but Yours be done." From that moment on, Jesus not only accepted that there was no other way to redeem mankind but through the cross, but He also set the ultimate example for us in how we are to deal with suffering. Adhering to God's will.

In our arrogance, we often say that God does not will for us to suffer. We quote the passage "For I know the plans I have for you," declares the LORD, "plans to prosper you and not to harm you, plans to give you hope and a future (Jeremiah 29:11, NIV)" and cite God's loving kindness, among other things, to support this claim. I don't think this is an accurate interpretation, as it ignores…frankly the Bible in entirety.

Let's have some examples. Job. Job was the richest man in the entire world, but he was also the godliest. Despite Job's righteousness, God wanted him to suffer so that God might refine Job to be an even better man, fully dependent upon God and to provide for you and me a stellar example of the purpose and plan God has through our suffering. Were there other motives? Probably, but the important motive to latch your mind on is that God allowed Job to suffer because Job's suffering brought God glory.

Jeremiah. Jeremiah was a young man when he started his ministry, probably no older than 30 years old, and he was, quite possibly, considerably younger. The man was laughed at and ignored by his entire nation. Jeremiah is known as the weeping prophet because he mourned how foolish his own nation was in rejecting the word that God had given him. However, God wanted this to happen so that He could show His might and power and discipline His children, Israel.

Jonah. Jonah was a reluctant prophet of God. He disobeyed God and ran away on a boat, but he could not escape God, because He caused a storm to rage against his boat, and Jonah knew that the only way to save the other sailors was for him to be tossed off the boat. We see at the end of the book of Jonah that he fled and had a bad attitude because he knew, he KNEW that God would forgive the Ninevites. Jonah did not want them to be forgiven because Nineveh, capital of the Assyrian Empire, was a corrupt, brutal, and cruel city, where the war machine that was the Assyrian army committed, what we would now call "war crimes" against every city they conquered. By making Jonah suffer, God turned an entire city to repentance. Ironic that the most corrupt city in the world would listen to the prophet of a foreign God, but Israel, who had dozens of prophets from God, warning them of destruction, would not truly listen to a single one.

The point is (you were waiting for this, weren't you?), God puts people through trials so that, ultimately, He may be glorified. This is but the primary reason, as I see it. The secondary reason we suffer is for our own benefit. Depending on how we act during the suffering our experiences will make us better people. It removes the false pretenses that we had about this world being so grand and great, and it makes us realize that Heaven is so much better than anything this world could possibly offer. That is the hope that Paul was talking about. We have the hope, the educated, reasonable assumption, that, even though this life can be agonizing, painful, heart-wrenching and uncaring, Heaven is going to be amazing.

When we think along these lines, not only do we get an increased desire to go Home, but, if we allow trials to do the work in us that is intended, we will become more like Jesus. It's kinda like this. I know some guys (well, really, I've seen it on TV) who can take a chunk of wood and start widdling away, and, after an hour or two, the chunk of wood turns into a chipmunk. Fascinating as it is for us to watch, I'm pretty sure the chunk of wood was not ecstatic about having a dull knife rip through its woody exterior. However, the craftsman knew what he was doing. He had an idea in mind, and made the worthless chunk of wood into a beautiful...well, at least, interesting-looking chipmunk.

In much the same way, God crafts us. Only, instead of crafting us like a chunk of wood, He molds us like a sword. First, He takes a long bar of steel, puts it into a raging hot furnace to make it malleable, and He then begins to pound it into shape. When the sword is of appropriate strength and shape, He begins to grind out an edge, paring away useless metal, filing away dull edges, and making a sharp sword.

In our lives, we face trials of the furnace, of the hammer, and of the file. The furnace melts down our resistance to God as we say to Him, "Alright, Your will be done." After He has been given permission to work further, He will pick up His hammer and begin to pound us into shape to look like His original model. In other words, after we have submitted to His will, God proceeds to hammer out everything that does not look like Jesus. When the work of the hammer is complete, God picks up a file and begins to file away all of the rough edges that were meant to be smooth, and creates a sharp edge, so that we might be of greater use and value to Him.

In the end, the trials we go through are intense, painful, and seemingly endless. But it is necessary if we are going to become like Jesus; more loving, more gracious, more humble, and more like a servant. In other words, trials make us into the kind of human beings that we were supposed to be. Of course, perfection will never be reached this side of eternity, but on the other side...golly, I can't wait to see what's going to happen.

Of course, any talk of trials and pain has to inevitably talk about the greatest of human griefs: death.

Man was warned in the Garden of Eden that disobedience to God would result in death. Man, of course, disobeyed and we therefore die. This next idea is not discussed in the Bible – or anywhere else that I am aware of – but I am convinced that it is true. Mankind is afraid of death, because we were not created to die. We were created to "serve God and obey His commands," and to walk with Him in the Garden of Eden but, since we neither served God nor obeyed

His commands, we went from immortality to mortality. Forced to walk this earth, toiling for our bread and struggling in the birthing process. Mankind's curse.

Then Jesus came, "born of a woman, born under the Law, to redeem those who were under the Law" and to "release those who, through fear of death were all their lifetimes subject to bondage," thus fulfilling the prophecy, "O Death, where is your sting? O Hades, where is your victory?"

It is quite simple, really. Death holds no power over the Christian. Instead, death should be viewed as the train that takes us home, because, as Paul described death, "We are confident, yes, well pleased rather to be absent from the body and to be present with the Lord (2 Cor. 5:8)." Death for the Christian is not supposed to hold fear or terror, because death is the vehicle by which we leave our pilgrimage on this world and begin to really live life in the next. We go from being separated from God to being in His presence daily. This is a vital element that is absent from the thoughts of today's Christian. We do not long for death as we ought, but instead, we fear death.

We may not admit it; we may put on a brave face to show the world, but we know deep inside that we are scared spitless of the idea that we will someday die. I believe that our fear comes from three forces working against us: a lack of faith, our own ignorance, and the scheme of the Enemy to make sure that the first two forces paralyze us with uncertainty and anxiety.

When I first started to have health problems, I was scared. I was young and I didn't want to die. I had too much life to live. It took several years, many books, and a lot of prayer before I could finally look forward to death and still try to live life as enthusiastically as possible. You see, it's not just about embracing the inevitability of death; it's about embracing the joy of life until death takes us Home.

Ironically (or not), the Devil has used the same schemes for thousands of years, but mankind has remained relatively ignorant, most of the time. C.S. Lewis in his brilliant work, *The Screwtape Letters*, showed us a glimpse of what the Devil might be planning and plotting for us to keep us away from Christ.

In the story, a senior tempter-demon named Screwtape who is writing letters of advice to his nephew Wormwood, who is a junior tempter-demon. One of these letters shows Screwtape telling Wormwood that mankind has been taught by the devil to view death as the prime evil and survival as the greatest good.

Ever since we were six years old and our goldfish died, we have all known that we were going to die. Granted, at the time we did not know what death meant. Heck, some of us still don't. Either way, we know that, at some point in time, the existence in which we currently dwell will cease to exist. However, because we are afraid of the unknown of death, we try to bottle it up, forget it will happen, and we treat death like a rude family member; by ignoring it and instead focus on living, hoping that death will never come.

When death happens - and it always does - we find ourselves shocked, hurt, fearful, and sad when someone close to us dies. If we are not sure of the existence of Heaven, we weep for the dead who we will never see again, and if we are sure of Heaven's existence and are reasonably convinced that our loved one is going there, we weep for ourselves instead because we will miss them.

Forgive what may seem harsh and cruel, but this is unbiblical and dangerous to us if we grieve excessively for the death of a saved loved one. In the early days of the church, it was considered a joyous thing when a brother or sister went to be with the Lord. The apostles braced themselves for it and were prepared to enter Heaven with jubilation.

The modern Church no longer holds such joyful views of death, but instead plays funeral dirges, and mourns the tears of the hopeless, even while we lie to ourselves and believe that we will see the dead again someday.

Am I showing a distinct lack of compassion to those that are hurting? No, in fact, I am trying to help them as best I can: by telling them to stop hurting. Guys, if you had a loved one die and they are a believer, then do not mourn for them, for they are in Heaven, and do not mourn for yourself, because that is just plain silly. You will see them soon enough.

Remember Job. Even without the certainty of Heaven, even without the freedom of redemption through Christ, Job had the right attitude towards death.

"Then Job arose, tore his robe, and shaved his head; and he fell to the ground and *worshipped*. And he said: 'Naked I came from my mother's womb, and naked shall I return there. The Lord gave, and the Lord has taken away; blessed be the name of the Lord [emphasis mine].'" (Job 1:20-21)

Job was sad, grieved, if you will, but he knew his priority was to worship, for God has a plan in mind that we cannot yet perceive. If you look at the book of Job, God does not explain Himself anywhere to Job. Job never received the answers he was looking for as to why he suffered because, rather than engage Job in an argument about what was or was not best, God simply said: "Who is this that darkens My council with words without knowledge? Now prepare yourself like a man; I will question you and you will answer me." (Job 38:2-3) God's entire answer to Job (summed up in three chapters) is that "I am God, you are not. My ways are above your ways, and for the time being, you are going to have to deal with the fact that I am not going to give you the answers you seek."

You probably do not know why your mother had to come down with leukemia and die, or why your child was hit by a drunken driver. But God does, and God's plan is so amazing that we can only stand in awe as we watch parts of it unfold. Even the tragedies, like the Holocaust or 9/11 have a purpose in God's eternal plan.

The Holocaust happened so that the nation of Israel would be reformed, according to prophecy. 9/11 could have happened so that the armies of Iraq would be eradicated so that they could not attack Israel, in accordance with another prophecy in Ezekiel. God has a plan for everything, but we, in our temporal mindsets can only speculate what that purpose is.

Maybe your mother died so that someone that came to the funeral would be saved. Maybe your son perished so young so that God could reveal to you that life is short and precious and that you must, you MUST treasure every moment that you have and live for Him. Or maybe, just maybe, the reason your husband died before he could see his newborn baby is because God just wanted him to come home.

What about yourself? What do you do when you are dying of cancer or you find yourself paralyzed from the waist down because of a car wreck? Every human is plagued by their own mortality, and honestly, I wish that people faced their mortality more often. As Lewis said, "God whispers to us in our pleasures, talks to us in our consciences, but shouts at us in our pain; it is His megaphone to a deaf world." Never is the Christian more inclined to rely on God than when he realizes that he cannot rely on himself.

Whether you are sick as a dog or healthy as an ox, I pray that you will always remember some other words of Job. After everything he owned and loved had been stripped from him and after his body was racked with a horrible disease Job said, "For I know that my Redeemer lives, and He shall stand at last on the earth; and after my skin is destroyed, this I know, that in my flesh I shall see God, whom I shall see for myself and my eyes shall behold, and not another. *How my heart yearns within me* [emphasis mine, although I'm sure Job would not object]!" (Job 19:25-27)

May your heart yearn within you to see God.
May you never fear death, for it is not an end, but a beginning.

Epilogue

This book is now at an end. My musings are finished.
Thanks for reading. God bless, and Jesus loves you.

Appendix:
How to Become a Christian

If you are reading this book and are not saved, then I hope that you have become interested in this systems of beliefs called Christianity. I hope that I have somehow managed to impress upon you that Jesus, the Son of God, loves you so much that He would leave Heaven, come to Earth, suffer and die in your stead, and then rise again to give you hope for the future.

I hope that the Holy Spirit is talking to you, even now, saying "Listen. Hear. This is important to you."

Here's the deal. You and I are sinners.

For us to "sin" is for us to act contrary to God's will and to disobey His Law. You've probably heard most of the ten commandments:

1. You shall have no other gods before God
    (Not TV stars, not possessions, and certainly not yourself)

2. You shall not make an image to worship any god.
    (No substitutes for God; you cannot let materialism become your god.)

3. You shall not take the name of the Lord in vain.
    ("Jesus Christ" is not a curse word. He is a person and He is God. His name deserves respect.)

4. Remember the Sabbath Day and keep it holy.
   (God declared that men should rest and not be consumed with working.)

5. Honor your father and mother.
   (Those that raised you when you were young deserve your help when they are old.)

6. You shall not murder.
   (Jesus went on to say that the thoughts of one's mind can be equivalent to murder.)

7. You shall not commit adultery.
   (Not with another man's wife, not with another woman's husband.)

8. You shall not steal.
   (Or pirate music, movies, games, etc.)

9. You shall not lie.
   (Even a little white lie.)

10. You shall not covet anything that is someone else's.
    (If you look at another person and long for anything that they have, be it their wife, be it their car, be it their bank account, you are coveting.)

These are the ten commandments, and if you have broken one commandment, you have broken them all (James 2:10). By breaking a commandment, you are sinning.

God is perfect and cannot allow sin to stand in His presence, so when you die, you are going to go to Hell. But that's not where the story ends. Hope is not forgotten, because you have been given a chance.

God became Man in the person of Jesus and lived among us. When He died, He took the guilt of all of your sin upon Himself. You see, sin demands punishment. Someone has to die for sin. Jesus decided that the death would be His.

Since He had lived a sinless life, He was able to absorb all of our guilt and all of our pain when He was dying. It's amazing to think that God's solution to our problem was to personally accept the guilt for our rebellion against Him and take that punishment Himself. That's how much He loves you and me.

After He died, He was buried. He rose from the dead three days later, and when His work on earth was complete, He simply rose into Heaven.

So how do you become a Christian?

It's really simple. You pray to God for forgiveness.

I'll walk you through it. Don't worry.

"God, forgive me, please, for I'm a sinner. I know that You died to take away my sins from me. Please forgive me. Please wash me clean of my sins. Until now, I have been the master of my own life, and now I ask that You take that position. Be my Lord and my Master. Teach me about You that I may know You more and love You.

Thank you, so much.

Amen."

And there are all the elements that you need to be saved. Confess your sin, ask for forgiveness, ask Jesus to be the uncontested Master of your life, and you'll be saved from Hell and from living a life in slavery to sin.

I now advise you to buy a Bible. My preference is called "Nelson's NKJV Study Bible" because it is in an easy-to-understand language, and, at the bottom of each page is an explanation of the text based on history and on other parts of the Bible (the author has not been paid to make this advertisement). It's a really good tool to have.

Find a church that will welcome you in and teach to you from the Bible. If the church is not welcoming; leave. If it does not teach from the Bible; leave. You need to be around people who will love you and you need to grow from hearing the Bible spoken.

Finally, when you find this church, consider being baptized. You have been saved of your sins; your old self has died and a new you has been born. Baptism is simply a public expression of an inward change. It is not necessary for you to be saved, but it is important for you to make a public declaration that you are not ashamed to be a Christian.

Welcome to a new life. Welcome to the Family. I hope to meet you in Heaven someday.